D1555599

Wild

France Royer &
Richard Dickinson

flowers

of *Calgary*

and Southern
Alberta

The
University
of Alberta
Press

Published by
The University of Alberta Press
Athabasca Hall
Edmonton, Alberta
Canada T6G 2E8

Printed in Canada   5 4 3 2 1

ISBN 0–88864–283–0

Canadian Cataloguing in Publication Data

Royer, France, 1951–
    Wildflowers of Calgary and Southern Alberta

    Includes bibliographical references and index.
    ISBN 0–88864–283–0

    1. Wild flowers—Alberta—Calgary—Identification. 2. Wild flowers—
Alberta—Calgary. 3. Wild flowers—Alberta—Identification. 4.Wild flowers—
Alberta. I. Dickinson, Richard, 1960– II. Title.
    QK203.A4R687 1996   582.13′097123′38   C96–910679–3

Color separations and filmwork by Resistance Graphics/Screaming Color,
Edmonton, Canada.
Printed and bound by Quality Color Press, Edmonton, Canada.
∞ Printed on acid-free paper.

COMMITTED TO THE DEVELOPMENT OF CULTURE AND THE ARTS

The publisher gratefully acknowledges the assistance of the Department of
Canadian Heritage.

WARNING

*The uses of plants discussed in this field guide are not in any way recommendations
by the authors or the publisher. Readers are cautioned against using these plants as
food or for self-medication. Notes about potential plant toxicity or irritating side
effects have been highlighted in the following descriptions, but we recommend
caution with ALL plants, especially those unfamiliar to you.*

Table of Contents

In Memory of Steven Joseph Toth

Acknowledgements

*T*he authors would like to thank friends and family who provided moral support and encouragement throughout the production of this field guide.

western Canada violet (page 99)

above: prickly pear (page 27)
opposite: common stonecrop (page 98)

Foreword

*R*ichard Dickinson and France Royer have produced a welcome addition to the growing list of botanical field guides. *Wildflowers of Calgary and Southern Alberta* has an attractive format and is easy to read, with descriptions of more than 100 flowering plants and with good colour photographs by France Royer. These photographs add immeasurably to the value of the book because they help to identify the flowers, one of the authors' main objectives. There are two photographs for most species; one shows the growth habit and the other gives a close-up of the flower. These close-ups are excellent and often reveal the detailed structure of the flower.

The notes under the 'Did you know?' headings are quite informative: they include how the plant got its name, traditional, commercial and medicinal uses of the species, and notes about toxicity and edibility.

Botanists will find the book interesting and will be glad to note that along with the common name of the plant, the scientific name (genus and species) is given, as well as the author's name. "Authors" are the scientists who name the plants and their names are so often omitted.

Flower-lovers living in southern Alberta, from Red Deer to the Montana border, will welcome this book.

Mrs. Beryl Hallworth
Calgary Field Naturalists' Society

top: running club-moss (page 59)
bottom left: clustered broom-rape (page 19)
bottom right: blue-eyed grass (page 51)
opposite: moss phlox (page 81)

Introduction

Wildflowers of Calgary and Southern Alberta is a handy field guide to plants found within the City of Calgary and across southern Alberta. The southern Alberta region is predominantly prairie grassland, with foothills and mountains to the west. This range of habitats features more than 1000 species of plants, large and small, including many showy wildflowers.

Forty-five plant families, with descriptions of 160 common or characteristic species, are included in this field guide. A simple identification key allows naturalists of all ages to recognize common features easily; line drawings are included to aid identification. Descriptions explain when and where to look for a plant, its identifying features and closely related species. Two hundred and five colour photographs complement the descriptions.

Plants in this guide are grouped in families, listed alphabetically by common family name. Within each family, species are listed alphabetically by scientific name but also identified by common names. Species belonging to the same family share similar characteristics, such as flower structure and leaf arrangement.

Species featured in this book can be viewed while traveling throughout the region, whether walking, cycling or hiking. An ethnobotanical section, included for most species, explains how plants were used by natives and early European settlers, and how they are used today. The guide is designed to be both informative and entertaining, encouraging readers to learn more about the ecology of southern Alberta.

WARNING

The uses of plants discussed in this field guide are not in any way recommendations by the authors or the publisher. Readers are cautioned against using these plants as food or for self-medication. Notes about potential plant toxicity or irritating side effects have been highlighted in the following descriptions, but we recommend caution with ALL plants, especially those unfamiliar to you.

Map of
Southern Alberta

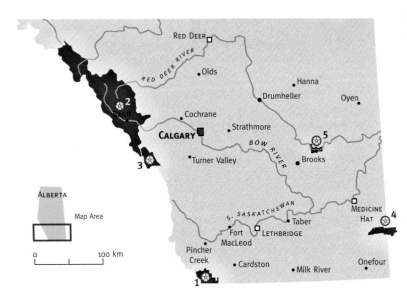

1 WATERTON LAKES NATIONAL PARK
2 BANFF NATIONAL PARK
3 KANANASKIS COUNTRY
4 CYPRESS HILLS
5 DINOSAUR PROVINCIAL PARK

Where to Find Wildflowers in Southern Alberta

THE CITY OF CALGARY

The City of Calgary boasts more than 6.8 km² of park and recreation area. Many of the parks are located in the Bow River and Elbow River valleys. Two large parks, Fish Creek Provincial Park and Nose Hill Park, are great areas for viewing wildflowers and wildlife. Fish Creek Provincial Park, located in southwest Calgary, covers an area of 1.2 km² and is a mix of grassland and deciduous forest. Nose Hill Park, on the north side of the city, rises 150 m above the Bow River. It is predominantly fescue grassland with small pockets of trembling aspen, chokecherry and saskatoon.

WATERTON LAKES NATIONAL PARK

Waterton Lakes National Park is located in the extreme southwest corner of Alberta. Established as an international peace park in 1932, it has over 183 km of backcountry trails with elevations ranging from 950 to 3200 m above sea level. Waterton Lakes National Park covers an area of 518 km² and boasts more than 1000 species of plants growing in a variety of habitats from prairie grassland to alpine slopes.

BANFF NATIONAL PARK

Banff National Park, founded in 1885, is located on the east side of the Rocky Mountains, west of Calgary. The park, an area of 6594 km², has hundreds of kilometres of hiking and backcountry trails. Habitats, ranging from montane forests to alpine slopes, allow more than 1000 species of plants to grow.

KANANASKIS COUNTRY

Kananaskis Country, which includes Peter Lougheed Provincial Park and Bow Valley Provincial Park, is located along the Continental Divide, south of Banff National Park. It covers over 4000 km², with habitats ranging from prairie grassland to alpine slopes. Over 800 species of plants have been identified from this region.

CYPRESS HILLS

The Cypress Hills are located on the border between Alberta and Saskatchewan, southeast of Medicine Hat, and cover an area of 2500 km². The maximum elevation of 1460 m is more than 600 m above the surrounding prairie. Several plant species of the foothills and Rocky Mountains can also be found here.

DINOSAUR PROVINCIAL PARK

Dinosaur Provincial Park, southeast of Drumheller, covers 90 km² of prairie grassland and badlands topography along the Red Deer River. The eroded slopes expose layers of sandstone and mudstone that few plants are capable of inhabiting.

PRAIRIE GRASSLAND

The Prairie Grassland region covers approximately 92,000 km² or 14% of the total area of the province. The dominant vegetation in this drought-prone area is grass, which comprises a large percentage of the 700 species that grow here. Broadleaf plants tend to flower in April, May and June while moisture is available.

Plant Structures

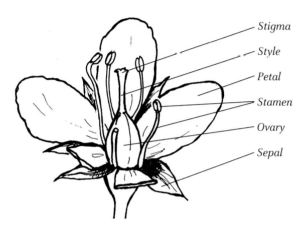

CROSS-SECTION OF A FLOWER

- *Stigma*
- *Style*
- *Petal*
- *Stamen*
- *Ovary*
- *Sepal*

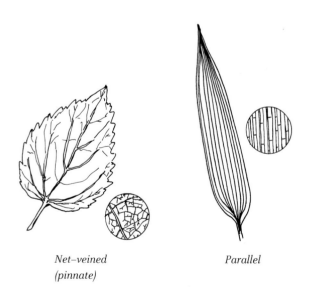

*Net–veined
(pinnate)*

Parallel

LEAF VENATION

Simple

*Palmately
Compound*

*Trifoliately
Compound*

*Pinnately
Compound*

LEAF TYPE

How to Use this Key

Answer question 1 *(page xvii)* to determine which leaf arrangement the plant exhibits. Proceed to the table or page number listed below the corresponding line drawing.

STEP 2

Select the appropriate habitat, growth habit or number of leaves as indicated in the first column of the table.

STEP 3

Choose the distinguishing characteristics that best describe the plant.

STEP 4

Proceed to the page numbers listed after the family name and compare the specimen with the photographs and text on those pages.

Note: Remember not all species are included in this field guide.

top left: old man's whiskers (page 91)
top right: smooth blue beard-tongue (page 39)
bottom left: star-flowered Solomon's-seal (page 57)
bottom right: toadflax (page 37)

Key to Plant Families

QUESTION 1

Which leaf arrangement does your plant exhibit?

ALTERNATE
Tables 1, 2, 3
Pages xviii–xxi

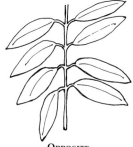

OPPOSITE
Table 4
Page xxii

BASAL
Table 6
Page xxiv

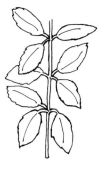

WHORLED
Table 5
Page xxiii

Plants with Alternate Leaves

Does your plant have a soft or woody stem?

Soft Stems – *see Table 1 or 2: Herbaceous Plants.*

Woody Stems – *see Table 3: Woody Plants.*

Are the leaves compound or simple?

Simple Leaves – *see Table 1.*

Compound Leaves – *see Table 2.*

TABLE 1

Herbaceous Plants with Alternate Simple Leaves

Leaf	Distinguishing Characteristics	Family (page #)
simple	petals 3 or less; plants with milky juice	*Spurge (97)*
	petals 3 or less, yellow; leaves plaited	*Orchid (69–71)*
	petals 4, pink or yellow; flowers more than 2 cm across	*Evening Primrose (34–35)*
	petals 4, pink; flowers less than 2 cm across	*Mustard (65–66)*
	petals 4, yellow; flowers less than 2 cm across	*Goosefoot (42)*
	petals 4, yellow; leaves succulent	*Stonecrop (98)*
	petals 5, blue; plant densely hairy	*Borage (18)*
	petals 5, blue, not united; leaves narrow	*Flax (40)*
	petals 5, blue, united; flowers bell-shaped; leaves narrow	*Harebell (44)*
	petals 5, orange to red; leaves greyish green	*Mallow (61)*
	petals 5, pink; leaves scale-like; plants pinkish brown	*Broomrape (19)*
	petals 5, pink; leaves floating on water	*Buckwheat (20–21)*

Leaf	Distinguishing Characteristics	Family (page #)
	petals 5, purple or red; flowers tube-shaped	*Figwort (36–39)*
	petals 5, yellow; flowers tube-shaped	*Figwort (36–39)*
	petals 5, yellow; plants aquatic	*Bladderwort (17)*
	petals 5, yellow; leaves greyish green; plants shrubby	*Goosefoot (42)*
	petals 5, yellow; leaves succulent	*Stonecrop (98)*
	petals 5, white, in terminal clusters; leaves narrow	*Sandalwood (96)*
	petals 5, white; leaves arrow-shaped; climbing plants	*Morning Glory (64)*
	petals 5, white; leaves heart-shaped	*Violet (99)*
	petals 5, white; leaves needle-shaped; dry prairie	*Phlox (81)*
	petals 6; flowers orange or white; leaves parallel-veined	*Lily (52–58)*
	petals 6; flowers green or yellow;leaves parallel-veined	*Orchid (69–71)*
	petals numerous, appearing in heads	*Aster (2–15)*
	petals numerous, red, pink or yellow, appearing leaf-like	*Figwort (36–39)*

TABLE 2
Herbaceous Plants with Alternate Compound Leaves

Leaf	*Distinguishing Characteristics*	*Family (page #)*
compound	flowers pea-shaped; various colors; fruit a pod	*Pea (72–80)*
	flowers yellow; plants aquatic	*Bladderwort (17)*
	flowers appearing in umbrella-shaped clusters	*Carrot (28)*
	plants hairy; seeds with hooked prickles; flowers yellow	*Rose (87–95)*
	plants not hairy; flowers white, pink or bronze	*Buttercup (22–26)*

TABLE 3
Woody Plants with Alternate Leaves

Growth Habit	Distinguishing Characteristics	Family (page #)
shrub	leaves compound; flowers white, pink or yellow	*Rose (87 95)*
	leaves compound; flowers yellow, pea-shaped	*Pea (72–80)*
	leaves simple; flowers white or yellow	*Rose (87–95)*
	leaves simple, silver-coloured; flowers yellow, appearing in leaf axils	*Oleaster (67–68)*
	leaves simple, lobed; stems with prickles; flowers white	*Currant (30)*
	leaves simple, evergreen; flowers pink	*Heath (45)*
	leaves simple, jagged edges; flowers appearing before the leaves	*Birch (16)*
	leaves simple, greyish green; flowers yellow, in terminal clusters	*Goosefoot (42)*
	leaves simple, greyish green; flowers yellow, appearing in heads	*Aster (2–15)*
tree	leaves needle-like, evergreen	*Pine (82)*
	leaves broad, deciduous	*Willow (100–102)*

TABLE 4
Plants with Opposite Leaves

Habitat	Distinguishing Characteristics	Family (page #)
climbing vine	leaves compound, 3 or 5 leaflets; flowers blue	Buttercup (22–26)
	leaves simple; flowers orange to red	Honeysuckle (46–49)
soft stems	leaves lobed; flowers white; plants hairy	Geranium (41)
	leaves not lobed; flowers pink; plants with milky juice	Dogbane (31)
	leaves not lobed; flowers yellowish, nodding; plants of mud flats	Aster (2–15)
	leaves not lobed; flowers pink or purple; stems square	Mint (62–63)
	leaves not lobed, whorl of 4 to 6 leaves below flower; flowers white	Dogwood (32–33)
woody stems	flowers white; petals 4; bark red	Dogwood (32–33)
	flowers white; petals 5; moss-like plants of dry open areas	Phlox (81)
	flowers white; petals 5; shrubs up to 2 m tall	Honeysuckle (46–49)
	flowers yellowish brown; petals 4; leaf underside brown-dotted	Oleaster (67–68)
	flowers yellow; petals 3 to 5; plants of dry open areas	Goosefoot (42)

TABLE 5
Plants with Whorled Leaves

Leaves Per Whorl	Distinguishing Characteristics	Family (page #)
2 to 5	flowers white or blue; leaves hairy	Buttercup (22–26)
4	flowers absent; plants moss-like	Little Club-moss (59)
4	flowers white; stems square	Madder (60)
4 to 6	flowers yellow; plants aquatic	Bladderwort (17)
4 to 6	flowers white with 4 large "petals"	Dogwood (32–33)
4 to 10	flowers yellow; plant of dry, open areas	Buckwheat (20–21)
5 to 8	flowers orange with black spots	Lily (52–58)
8 to 16	flowers absent; stems jointed and hollow	Horsetail (50)

TABLE 6
Plants with Basal Leaves

Leaf	Distinguishing Characteristics	Family (page #)
with hairs	leaves compound; flowers pink, usually 3	*Rose (87–95)*
	leaves compound; flowers yellow or blue, pea-shaped	*Pea (72–80)*
	leaves lobed; flowers yellow	*Aster (2–15)*
	leaves lobed; flowers white or blue	*Buttercup (22–26)*
	leaves simple; flowers yellow; petals 4	*Mustard (65–66)*
	leaves simple; flowers yellow; petals 6	*Buckwheat (20–21)*
	leaves simple; flowers white; petals 4	*Plantain (83)*
without hairs	flowers green; plants of wetland areas	*Cattail (29)*
	flowers blue; plants with grass-like leaves	*Iris (51)*
	flowers pink or white; plants with grass-like leaves	*Lily (52–58)*
	flowers pink or white; plants with leathery rounded leaves	*Wintergreen (103–104)*
	flowers pink, white or lilac; petals 5; plants of wetland or dry areas	*Primrose (84–86)*
	flowers white; stem with one small leaf	*Grass-of-Parnassus (43)*
	flowers yellowish; single inconspicuous leaf	*Orchid (69–71)*

Plant Descriptions

Individual plant descriptions follow on pages 2–104.

top: scarlet mallow (page 61)
bottom left: marsh hedge nettle (page 63)
bottom right: sparrow's-egg lady's-slipper (page 70)

yarrow

Achillea millefolium L.

WHERE, WHEN AND WHAT TO LOOK FOR

Yarrow commonly grows in prairie grassland, roadside ditches and waste areas throughout our region. Flower heads appear from **June to August.** They are composed of 10 to 30 yellow disc florets and 5 to 12 sterile, white or pinkish ray florets. The woolly-haired stem, which grows to 80 cm, has alternate leaves 4 to 15 cm long, feathered into numerous 1 to 2 mm wide segments (giving the species its name, *millefolium*, meaning 'thousand leaves'). The fruit is a flattened achene with no pappus.

DID YOU KNOW...

The genus *Achillea* is named after the Greek hero Achilles, who is said to have treated the wounds of his soldiers with yarrow. Natives and herbalists continued to use this herb medicinally. The Cree treated earaches, constipation, stomach ailments, burns and infections with yarrow. A tea made from yarrow and strawberries was taken to treat insanity. A yarrow shampoo was made to prevent baldness. Dried yarrow leaves and flowers added to a warm bath have been used to relieve arthritic pain.

common burdock

Arctium minus (Hill) Bernh.

WHERE, WHEN AND WHAT TO LOOK FOR

Common burdock was introduced from Europe and is now found in waste places, railway grades and edges of wooded areas throughout Alberta. Flowers appear from **July to August** as heads (1 to 3 cm thick) of pinkish purple disc florets enclosed in several series of bracts bearing hooked prickles. The plant grows to 2 m, with large basal leaves and alternate stem leaves that can grow up to 50 cm long and 40 cm wide. The leaf underside appears pale due to a mass of woolly hairs. The fruit, a small, dry, single seed, does not open when ripe. It is 5 to 6 mm long and has 3 to 5 angles and a bristly pappus. Each flowering head produces several single-seeded fruits.

DID YOU KNOW...

The Japanese cultivate burdock as a prized vegetable. The fleshy taproot of first-year plants, called 'Gobo', can be eaten raw or cooked. The root, ground and roasted, serves as a coffee substitute. The leaves, flowering stalks and seeds are all edible.

sagebrush

Artemisia cana Pursh

long-leaved sage

WHERE, WHEN AND WHAT TO LOOK FOR

Sagebrush, a shrub with twisted, gnarled stems, grows to a height of 150 cm on prairies, dry hillsides and eroded slopes of southern Alberta. Alternate leaves, 1 to 4 cm long, are silvery to pale gray. Small, yellow flowers, 1 to 2 mm long in groups of 5 to 20, appear on leafy, flowering stems in **July and August**.

SIMILAR SPECIES

A closely related species, long-leaved sage (*A. longifolia* Nutt.) grows alongside sagebrush. Unlike sagebrush, it has non-woody stems that grow from a woody base. Leaves, 5 to 10 cm long, have edges that are rolled under and towards the midrib. Small, yellow flowers (4 to 5 mm long) appear in August.

DID YOU KNOW...

The Blackfoot name for sagebrush is *ah-pu-tu-yis,* which means 'weasel grass'. Sagebrush leaves were chewed to relieve thirst. The seeds were eaten raw. Sagebrush was used by native peoples for livestock forage in fall and winter.

sagebrush

pasture sagewort
Artemisia frigida Willd.

plains wormwood

WHERE, WHEN AND WHAT TO LOOK FOR

Pasture sagewort is found on dry, south-facing riverbanks and overgrazed pastures and prairie. Small flower heads appear from **July to August.** They are composed of small, yellow disc florets enclosed by hairy bracts. The small flowers are hidden in the leafy, woody stalk, which can grow to a height of 50 cm. Alternate, silver-green leaves are 1 to 3 cm long, dissected into narrow segments. They give off the distinct scent of sage, especially when rubbed between the fingers. The fruit is an achene, 3 mm long and without a pappus.

SIMILAR SPECIES

A closely related species, plains wormwood (*A. campestris* L.), has reddish stems and is found in dry, sandy areas.

DID YOU KNOW...

Pasture sagewort has many uses. The Blackfoot chewed the leaves to relieve heartburn and used the leaves to brew a tea as a remedy for coughs and colds. Trappers used the aromatic leaves as bait in their traps. Leaves can be used as a stuffing or seasoning fresh or dried, and they add a natural perfume to sachets or pot-pourri. Leaves tossed into a campfire produce a pleasant fragrance.

pasture sagewort

Canada thistle

Cirsium arvense (L.) Scop.

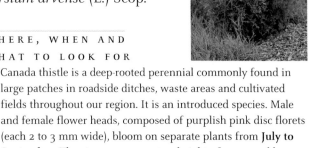

WHERE, WHEN AND WHAT TO LOOK FOR

Canada thistle is a deep-rooted perennial commonly found in large patches in roadside ditches, waste areas and cultivated fields throughout our region. It is an introduced species. Male and female flower heads, composed of purplish pink disc florets (each 2 to 3 mm wide), bloom on separate plants from **July to September.** The stems can grow to a height of 1.5 m and have alternate leaves 5 to 15 cm long with prickly lobed segments. The fruit is an achene with a white, feathery pappus.

DID YOU KNOW...

A plaster made from boiled thistle roots has been used as a deodorant. The cottony seeds have been stuffed into pillows, cushions and mattresses. The young leaves and roots of Canada thistle make an excellent vegetable. Livestock will eat Canada thistle when grass is scarce. Herbalists may prescribe thistle for treatment of muscle spasms, rickets and nervous disorders. Fresh-cut thistle flowers add a pleasant fragrance to a room, and dried flowers can be added to sachets and pot-pourris.

tufted fleabane

Erigeron caespitosus Nutt.

WHERE, WHEN AND WHAT TO LOOK FOR

Tufted fleabane, a deep-rooted perennial of prairie grassland and dry hillsides, can be found throughout southern Alberta. Plants, up to 25 cm tall, are greyish to olive-green due to short, stiff hairs that cover the plant surface. Stalked basal leaves are spatula-shaped, 2 to 8 cm long with 3 prominent veins. Stem leaves are stalkless, narrow and reduced in size near the top of the stem. There are 1 to 4 flower heads per stem, each with 3 to 4 rows of overlapping involucral bracts. Flower heads, 2 to 3 cm across, are composed of 30 to 100 white or pinkish ray florets (5 to 15 mm long) and numerous yellow disc florets (2 to 7 mm long). The fruit, an achene, has a pappus consisting of numerous bristles.

SIMILAR SPECIES

Twenty-four species of fleabane are found in Alberta. They grow in a variety of habitats, ranging from dry, open grassland to moist alpine slopes.

DID YOU KNOW...

The Plains peoples burned fleabane on the skin to relieve minor irritations.

gaillardia

Gaillardia aristata Pursh

WHERE, WHEN AND WHAT TO LOOK FOR

Gaillardia is common on prairie grassland, roadsides and dry, open areas of southern Alberta. Plants, up to 60 cm tall, have alternate, coarsely toothed or lobed leaves 5 to 12 cm long. The plant is covered with stiff, grey hairs, giving it a bristly texture. Flower heads are 3 to 7 cm across and appear in **July and August.** There are 10 to 18 outer, yellow ray florets, each 3-lobed and wedge-shaped. The center is composed of numerous crimson-coloured, hairy disc florets. The fruit is an achene and has a pappus of 5 to 10 short bristles.

SIMILAR SPECIES

Several species of gaillardia are grown as ornamentals. They are usually sold under the common name 'blanketflower'.

DID YOU KNOW...

The Blackfoot made a tea from the roots of gaillardia to treat stomach disorders. The tea was also used as an eyewash, for nose drops and as a bath for nursing mothers. The powdered roots were often applied to skin irritations.

golden aster, hairy golden aster

Heterotheca villosa

(Pursh) Shinners

WHERE, WHEN AND WHAT TO LOOK FOR

Golden aster is common in dry, open, sandy areas of central and southern Alberta. Another common name, hairy golden aster, refers to the bristly nature of the plant. Stems, up to 50 cm tall, rise from a woody rootstalk. Branches are nearly prostrate and have numerous alternate, stalkless leaves 2 to 5 cm long. Flower heads appear at the ends of branches in **July through September.** They are 25 to 30 mm across and composed of 15 to 35 bright-yellow ray florets and numerous disc florets. The ray florets are 6 to 10 mm long. The fruit, an achene, has a pappus consisting of rough hairs and minute bristles.

DID YOU KNOW ...

Golden aster can be distinguished from true asters by the colour of their florets. There are no native species of aster with yellow florets.

Colorado rubber-weed, Colorado rubber-plant

Hymenoxys richardsonii

(Hook.) Cockerell

WHERE, WHEN AND WHAT TO LOOK FOR

Colorado rubber-weed is common on the prairies and dry eroded slopes of southern Alberta. Rubber-weed grows up to 20 cm tall, with several stems rising from a thick, woody stalk. It is a perennial. Basal leaves, 5 to 10 cm long, are divided into 3 to 7 narrow divisions. Some alternate stem leaves are present. Yellow flower heads, 2 cm across, are composed of 3-lobed ray florets (7 to 10 mm long) and 5-lobed disc florets (3 to 4 mm long). The fruit, an achene, has 5 or 6 short bristles.

DID YOU KNOW...

The Blood people had several uses for this plant. The whole plant was used as a handkerchief by children. The plant's scent was used to cause sneezing and to clear the head of cold or headache. A dye was made to colour arrow shafts. The roots yield a rubbery substance that could be used as chewing gum. Colorado rubber-plant, as it is also known, is unpalatable to livestock and tends to increase in overgrazed pastures.

poverty-weed
Iva axillaris Pursh

WHERE, WHEN AND WHAT TO LOOK FOR

Poverty-weed, a perennial that spreads by underground roots, is common on saline clay flats, eroded slopes and lakeshores of southern Alberta. Stems, up to 50 cm tall, have thick leaves with 3 veins and are 1 to 3 cm long. Lower leaves are opposite, and upper leaves are alternate. Nodding flower heads, composed of 12 to 20 male and 5 to 8 female flowers, are borne in leaf axils. These small, greenish yellow flowers are 2 to 3 mm across. The fruit, an achene, is about 3 mm long. Poverty-weed grows as a weed where conditions are favourable.

SIMILAR SPECIES

A closely related species, false ragweed (*I. xanthifolia* Nutt.), is common in moist, open areas of southern Alberta. The leaves and stems of false ragweed resemble those of sunflowers; the flowers, however, are quite different. Stems have opposite leaves and can reach a height of 2 m.

pineapple-weed
Matricaria matricarioides
(Less.) Porter

pineapple-weed

WHERE, WHEN AND WHAT TO LOOK FOR

Pineapple-weed, an introduced species in our area, is common in waste areas, roadsides and yards. The greenish yellow, cone-shaped flower heads are composed of disc florets. Flower heads can be seen from **June through September.** The plant grows to a height of 40 cm, with numerous branches. Its alternate leaves (1 to 5 cm long) are each divided into several narrow segments. Pineapple-weed has a strong pineapple odour. The fruit is an achene without a hairy pappus.

SIMILAR SPECIES

A closely related species, scentless chamomile (*M. perforata* Mérat), has white ray florets and yellow disc florets. Its leaves are 2 to 8 cm long with narrower divisions than those of pineapple weed.

DID YOU KNOW...

A tea known for its relaxing effect can be brewed from the flower heads, leaves and stems of either species. Both species can be added to a hot bath for an aromatic soak. The Blackfoot used pineapple-weed as a perfume and an insect repellent.

scentless chamomile

mountain goldenrod

Canada goldenrod

Solidago canadensis L.

WHERE, WHEN AND WHAT TO LOOK FOR

Canada goldenrod, recognized by its bright-yellow flowers, is
common in areas ranging from open meadows to the edges of
aspen forests. Flower heads appear from **August through
September.** They are composed of ray florets, 3 to 6 mm long.
The flower cluster is usually pyramid-shaped. The plant grows
to 1.2 m, with numerous, alternate leaves 5 to 10 cm long, each
with 3 prominent veins. The fruit is an achene with bristly,
white hairs.

SIMILAR SPECIES

A closely related species, mountain goldenrod (*S. spathulata*
DC.), grows to 40 cm tall and is found throughout our region.
The flower cluster is cylindrical in shape and has bright-yellow
flowers.

DID YOU KNOW...

Goldenrod flowers make a bright-yellow dye. This plant was an
ingredient for astringents and diuretics, and was sometimes
claimed to be a treatment for diphtheria. Some natives treated
sore throats with a mixture made from grease and mashed goldenrod leaves. Young leaves are excellent when added to salads
or cooked like spinach.

*Canada
goldenrod*

tansy

Tanacetum vulgare L.

WHERE, WHEN AND WHAT TO LOOK FOR

Tansy was introduced from Europe as a garden flower, but thrived and became a weed. It is common in roadside ditches, waste areas and pastures. Each stem has over 200 button-shaped, yellowish orange flower heads (6 to 10 mm across) that bloom from **July through September.** The plant stem grows to 180 cm in height and has a pungent odour when crushed. Alternate leaves, up to 20 cm long, are pinnately divided into numerous segments. The fruit is an achene with small ridges and a reduced pappus.

DID YOU KNOW…

Tansy flowers release a strong aroma that repels insects. Early prairie farmers put the dried flowers in their grain bins to keep mice and other rodents away. Modern herbalists sometimes recommend this plant as a tonic for various internal disorders. A skin lotion can be made by soaking the young leaves in buttermilk for about 10 days. Tansy can be **toxic** to humans and caution should be exercised when using any part of this plant.

goat's-beard
Tragopogon dubius Scop.

WHERE, WHEN AND WHAT TO LOOK FOR

Goat's-beard is a weed introduced from the southwestern United States. It thrives in waste areas, roadside ditches and railway grades. Its flower heads bloom from **June through August.** They are composed of bright-yellow, ray florets (up to 6 mm across) and 10 to 14 green involucral bracts that are longer than the ray florets. The stem grows to 100 cm tall and has a fleshy taproot and milky sap, much like that of the dandelion. Alternate, grass-like leaves grow up to 30 cm in length. Its achenes, about 25 to 30 mm long, have a feather-like pappus, about 4 cm long. The fruiting head is usually 7 to 10 cm in diameter. The flowers of goat's-beard are sensitive to light and temperature. On sunny days the flowers follow the sun; they remain closed on cloudy days.

DID YOU KNOW...

The roots and leaves of this plant make a pleasant addition to salads. Some people say the cooked taproot tastes like parsnips or oysters. Early European settlers and some natives believed the milky juice dissolved gallstones. Drinking the juice moistens the mouth and is believed by some to promote good digestion.

green alder
Alnus crispa (Alt.) Pursh

green alder

WHERE, WHEN AND WHAT TO LOOK FOR

Green alder grows as a common shrub in sandhills, bogs and dry, open forests. It may reach a height of 3 m. Male and female flowers bloom in April in separate catkins; female flowers are pinkish purple, and male flowers are yellowish-brown. The female catkins, dry, cone-like structures 1 to 2 cm long, produce seeds and often remain on the stems for several seasons. Alternate, oval leaves, 2 to 8 cm long with coarsely serrated leaf margins, appear with the catkins in **early May.**

SIMILAR SPECIES

A closely related species, river alder (*A. tenuifolia* Nutt.), grows to 8 m and is found along river banks and lakeshores.

DID YOU KNOW...

The Blackfoot produced a yellow dye from the catkins of green alder and an orange or reddish brown dye from the inner bark. They boiled the bark with vinegar to make a mouthwash and an excellent remedy for lice. They also used the bark to add flavour to smoked fish and meat. They called the shrub *a-muck-ko-kytis* ('red-mouth bush') because chewing the inner bark turned the mouth red.

river alder with last year's catkins

common bladderwort
Utricularia vulgaris L.

WHERE, WHEN AND WHAT TO LOOK FOR

Common bladderwort, an insectivorous plant, can be found in lakes, streams and ponds throughout Alberta. This free-floating plant has submersed alternate or whorled, finely divided leaves with numerous, clear bladders. These bladders, 3 to 5 mm long, close when insects and small organisms enter, trapping them. The bladders also help keep the plant afloat and the flowers above the water surface. The only part of the plant visible at the surface is a yellow flower with red or brown stripes. The flower, 14 to 20 mm wide, rises on a slender stem above the water surface. Flowers appear in **June and July.** The fruit, a capsule, contains numerous, wrinkled seeds.

SIMILAR SPECIES

Three other species of bladderwort are found in Alberta: horned bladderwort (*U. cornuta* Michx), flat-leaved bladderwort (*U. intermedia* Hayne), and small bladderwort (*U. minor* L.). They are easily identified by their yellow flowers and underwater bladders.

DID YOU KNOW...

Bladderworts produce small green structures called winter buds. These winter buds sink to the bottom of the waterbody and germinate in the spring.

bluebur

Lappula squarrosa

(Retz.) Dumort.

WHERE, WHEN AND WHAT TO LOOK FOR

Bluebur, a weed introduced from Asia and Europe, inhabits waste areas, railway grades, gardens and roadsides. Its pale-blue flower (about 3 to 6 mm across) has a yellow throat and is borne in leafy clusters. It can be seen **June through September.** An annual or winter annual, this freely branching plant is hairy overall and can grow to a height of 50 cm. Its alternate, greyish green leaves are narrow and up to 7 cm long, with numerous stiff hairs. Each flower produces 4 fruits that appear as nutlets with 2 rows of prickles. Seeds are spread by the prickles, which hook themselves to fur and clothing.

DID YOU KNOW...

The genus name, *Lappula*, is Latin for 'small burs'.

clustered broom-rape
Orobanche fasciculata Nutt.

WHERE, WHEN AND WHAT TO LOOK FOR

Clustered broom-rape is a parasitic plant that attaches itself to the roots of other plants, primarily members of the Aster Family. It can be found on prairie grassland throughout southern Alberta. Clustered broom-rape has no chlorophyll and derives most nutrients from its host. Pinkish brown stems, up to 10 cm tall, have alternate, scale-like leaves and purplish, tube-shaped flowers. The fruit, a capsule, produces many microscopic seeds.

SIMILAR SPECIES

Two other species of broom-rape grow in Alberta: common broom-rape (*O. ludoviciana* Nutt.) and one-flowered cancer-root (*O. uniflora* L.). Both species have no chlorophyll, reduced leaves and small seeds, characteristics of parasitic plants.

DID YOU KNOW...

Plains peoples called clustered broom-rape 'sand-food', referring to the succulent, edible part of the plant underground. Its roots were often roasted in the campfire.

yellow umbrella-plant

Eriogonum flavum Nutt.

WHERE, WHEN AND WHAT TO LOOK FOR

Yellow umbrella-plant, common on dry plains and rocky outcrops, is found throughout southern Alberta. The plant rises to 30 cm tall from a woody rootstalk. Basal leaves, 2 to 5 cm long, are green above and have a white, woolly underside. A whorl of leaf-like bracts can be found below the flower cluster. Flowers, each 4 to 5 mm across, consist of 6 yellow sepals, 9 long-stalked stamens and 3 styles. Petals are absent. The fruit, an achene, is triangular and about 4 mm long.

DID YOU KNOW...

The stems of yellow umbrella-plant were brewed as a face wash to dry sores and reduce swelling. The roots were chewed and the resulting mash used for earplugs. Children often ate the roots like candy. Plains peoples mixed the flowers with brain, liver and spleen and applied the mixture to hides to bleach them.

yard knotweed

water smartweed, lady's-thumb

Polygonum amphibium L.

WHERE, WHEN AND WHAT TO LOOK FOR

Water smartweed, or lady's-thumb, can be found in the shallow water of sloughs, ditches and lakeshores throughout Alberta. Flowers appear in dense, cylindrical spikes (1 to 3 cm long) from **June through August.** Sepals are pink to reddish purple, 4 to 5 mm long; petals are absent. The water smartweed is a semi-aquatic plant. It sometimes emerges from the water on weak stems that seldom reach more than 35 cm. Dark-green, alternate leaves are oblong, 2 to 20 cm long and often floating. The fruit is a dry, lens-shaped seed, 2 to 4 mm in length.

SIMILAR SPECIES

A closely related species, yard knotweed (*P. arenastrum* Jord. ex Bor.), is a common weed in yards, waste places and roadsides. Sepals are green with white or pink margins. Petals are absent.

DID YOU KNOW...

The Cree applied the crushed fresh root of water smartweed to mouth blisters. Waterfowl, shorebirds and muskrats feed on water smartweed.

water smartweed

baneberry, snake-berry

Actaea rubra (Ait.) Willd.

WHERE, WHEN AND WHAT TO LOOK FOR

A common herb of aspen and mixed-wood forests, baneberry, or snake-berry, can be found in the northern and western parts of our region. White flowers bloom from **May to July.** They bear 4 to 10 petals and 3 to 5 sepals (which fall off after the flower opens). Flowers are 3 mm across and appear in cone-shaped clusters. Baneberry grows to 1 m and has 1 to 5 alternate compound leaves, each with 3 to 7 sharply toothed leaflets. Showy berries, red or white in colour with a black dot at the apex, are 6 to 10 mm in diameter. The berries are **poisonous**.

DID YOU KNOW ...

Although the berries are **poisonous**, other parts of the plant have been widely used. The Blackfoot boiled the root and used the resulting decoction as a cold remedy. A mixture of baneberry root and spruce needles was used to treat stomach ailments.

Berries may be red.

Canada anemone

Canada anemone

Anemone canadensis L.

WHERE, WHEN AND WHAT TO LOOK FOR

Canada anemone can be found in moist ditches and forested areas throughout Alberta. Its white flowers (2.5 to 3 cm across) bear 5 or 6 sepals (no petals). They bloom from **June to July**. Canada anemone rises from an underground stem to heights from 20 to 60 cm, depending on habitat. A whorl of leaves, 4 to 7 cm wide and deeply cleft into 3 to 5 divisions, is located below each flower. The fruit, a dry, brown, single-seeded achene, appears in globe-shaped clusters.

SIMILAR SPECIES

A closely related species, long-fruited anemone (*A. cylindrica* A. Gray), commonly grows in open, wooded areas and prairie grassland. The sepals are cream coloured and have a silky outer surface.

DID YOU KNOW...

The plains peoples used Canada anemone externally on sores. Anemones contain **caustic irritants** which can be harmful; do not consume, and handle carefully.

long-fruited anemone

prairie crocus, pasque-flower

Anemone patens L.

WHERE, WHEN AND WHAT TO LOOK FOR

The prairie crocus can commonly be found in open, lodgepole-pine forests, sand dunes and dry, prairie grassland. It is one of the earliest blooming plants in Alberta. The pale-blue flower has 5 to 7 petal-like sepals, but no petals. The sepals are 2 to 4 cm in length with silky hair on the outer surface. The feathery styles elongate by the time the plant's furry, greyish green leaves fully emerge, so seeds can be easily spread by the wind.

DID YOU KNOW...

Native lore refers to the prairie crocus as the 'ears of the earth' because it seems to spring through the snow to listen for the approach of summer. Native legends also tell of the Great Spirit giving this delicate plant a fur coat to keep it warm through cold spring nights. In fact, the hairs discourage insects and grazing animals. The Blackfoot used the plant for healing, making a poultice from the leaves to ease rheumatic pain. Early European settlers made a dye from the pale-blue sepals and used it to colour Easter eggs.

purple clematis
Clematis occidentalis
(Hornem.) DC.

WHERE, WHEN AND WHAT TO LOOK FOR

Purple clematis is common in open forests, shrubland and north-facing slopes. It is a twisting, semi-woody vine that grasps onto surrounding vegetation. In **May to late June**, single flowers with 4 to 6 blue sepals (1 to 6 cm long) and no petals appear on the long leaf stalks. After the flower fades, styles lengthen to form a dense head of feathery fruits that are easily spread by the wind. Leaves are composed of 3 leaflets, each 2 to 8 cm long. The vine can grow as long as 2 m.

SIMILAR SPECIES

A closely related, introduced species, yellow clematis (*C. tangutica* (Max.) Korsh.), prefers sunny, open areas along fence lines and edges of forests. It has yellow flowers and 5 leaflets, and resembles a yellow Chinese lantern, its other common name.

DID YOU KNOW ...

Protoam, a **poisonous** agent that causes respiratory paralysis, is found in purple clematis. This chemical is also found in other species of the Buttercup Family.

veiny meadow rue

Thalictrum venulosum Trel.

female flowers

WHERE, WHEN AND WHAT TO LOOK FOR

Veiny meadow rue is common in aspen forests and moist
prairies throughout Alberta. Male and female flowers, borne on
separate plants, bloom from **June through July**. The male flower
(6 to 10 mm long) consists of several yellow stamens. The
female flower (6 to 8 mm long) has many green to pinkish
purple pistils. Both flowers have 4 to 5 greenish white sepals
that fall off soon after blooming. Veiny meadow rue grows from
15 to 90 cm tall. It has yellow roots and alternate compound
leaves with 3 to 5 3-lobed leaflets. The leaflets, 2 to 3 cm across,
have a pale underside with dark veins. The fruits appear as a
cluster of ribbed achenes, 3 to 6.5 mm long.

SIMILAR SPECIES

Two other species of meadow rue can be found in southern
Alberta: tall meadow rue (*T. dasycarpum* Fisch. & Avé-Lall.) and
western meadow rue (*T. occidentale* A. Gray). Both species are
usually more robust than veiny meadow rue.

DID YOU KNOW...

The Blackfoot used the whole veiny meadow rue plant as a
source of perfume.

male flowers

prickly pear, cactus

Opuntia polyacantha Haw.

WHERE, WHEN AND WHAT TO LOOK FOR

Prickly pear, or cactus, is found on prairie grassland, eroded slopes and unvegetated areas of southern Alberta. The stem segments, often referred to as paddles, are 5 to 12 cm long and 1 cm thick. Each segment corresponds to a single season's growth. Leaves are small and fall off as new segments appear. Groups of 5 to 9 straight spines rise from small, hairy cushions called 'areolae'. Yellow flowers, 4 to 7 cm across, are composed of numerous sepals, petals, stamens and a single 5 to 7-lobed stigma. The edible fruit is about 3 cm long and spiny; it contains several flat seeds.

SIMILAR SPECIES

A closely related species, brittle prickly pear (*O. fragilis* (Nutt.) Haw.), can be found growing alongside prickly pear. It has smaller segments (2 to 5 cm long) with 3 to 7 spines per areola.

DID YOU KNOW...

To treat rheumatism, the Blackfoot inserted cactus spines into the flesh of the patient. The spines were then set afire and burnt to the surface of the skin. Cactus flower buds can be roasted and eaten as a vegetable. Syrup, jelly or candy can be made from the fruit.

cow parsnip

Heracleum lanatum Michx.

WHERE, WHEN AND WHAT TO LOOK FOR

Cow parsnip is common in moist forests and open meadows throughout Alberta . White flowers (up to 6 mm across) bloom in umbels, from **June to August**. Petals are of varying sizes; the largest flowers appear on the edge of the umbel. Alternate leaves grow up to 30 cm wide and are composed of 3 lobed and prominently veined leaflets. The hollow, hairy stem grows up to 2.5 m tall. The fruit is small (up to 1 cm long), dry and flattened, with visible lines on its sides.

DID YOU KNOW...

Cow parsnip belongs to the carrot family, as do caraway and dill. Young cow parsnip roots can be cooked like ordinary parsnips. Cow parsnip seeds add flavour to soups and stews. The peeled leaf stalk can be eaten fresh, but **take care** because the peel contains a chemical that can blister skin. A drink made from the roots or seeds was sometimes taken to relieve asthma, colic, colds and cramps.

cattail
Typha latifolia L.

WHERE, WHEN AND WHAT TO LOOK FOR

The cattail, a common marsh plant found along ditches and on the margins of sloughs and lakes throughout Alberta, is frequently overlooked as one of North America's edible wild plants. It has 2 types of flowers, male and female, both lacking petals and sepals. The male flowers are borne in a greenish brown terminal spike, 8 to 15 cm long and about 2 cm in diameter. The female flowers are borne in a brown spike, 4 to 5 cm in diameter, located about 1 cm below the male spike. Several basal leaves, each 1 to 3 cm wide and up to 50 cm long, rise from the large, creeping root system. By **mid-August**, the female spike contains thousands of tiny fruits covered with white hair.

DID YOU KNOW ...

Young female cattail flowers can be boiled and eaten like corn on the cob. Male flowers can be dried, ground and used to extend equal amounts of flour in baking. Roots can be boiled and used as a low-fat, equal-protein substitute for rice, corn and potatoes. The Blackfoot applied cattail fluff as an antiseptic to burns and scalds. The Cree chopped and ate the stems to relieve diarrhea. The spongy, olive-green leaves can be woven into baskets and mats. Fluff from the female spike can be gathered in the fall and used as pillow stuffing or insulating material. It was used extensively during World War I to stuff life jackets.

common gooseberry
Ribes oxyacanthoides L.

WHERE, WHEN AND WHAT TO LOOK FOR

Look for the common gooseberry in moist areas of aspen and balsam-poplar forests, and occasionally in white-spruce stands. It is found throughout Alberta. Clusters of flowers appear in leaf axils from **May through June**. Flowers (4 to 5 mm long) bear 5 greenish white sepals (curved backwards) and 5 white or greenish, bell-shaped petals. The shrub grows up to 2 m. Many prickles cluster at the bases of its alternate leaves. Leaves are maple-leaf-shaped, 3 to 5-lobed and 3 to 5 cm across. Branches become less prickly as they mature. Gooseberry fruit matures to reddish purple and measures 10 to 15 mm in diameter.

SIMILAR SPECIES

A closely related species, golden currant (*R. aureum* Pursh) is a common shrub found growing on riverbanks and rocky slopes in southern Alberta. Its leaves are 3 to 5-lobed. Its bright-yellow flowers often have a reddish tinge.

DID YOU KNOW...

The Blood people ate boiled gooseberry leaves with sugar. An extract from the roots deodorizes hair, smelly feet and general body odour. The gooseberry fruit contains citric acid and pectin, making it a good choice for jelly.

spreading dogbane

Apocynum androsaemifolium L.

WHERE, WHEN AND WHAT TO LOOK FOR

Spreading dogbane is common in habitats ranging from dry, sandy areas to open forests. Fragrant, pinkish white flowers (6 mm long) bloom from **June through August.** The bell-shaped corolla has dark-pink lines on the inside and is formed by the union of 5 petals. Flowers are borne at the ends of reddish green stems that contain a milky-white juice. Stems can grow to a height of 1 m but are more common at 50 cm. Bright-green, opposite leaves, 2.5 to 7.5 cm in length, turn golden-yellow to red in the autumn. **Poisonous fruit** forms in late July, in pairs of reddish-green pods, 2 to 10 cm long. Other parts of the plant may also be **poisonous**: do not consume.

DID YOU KNOW...

Because of dogbane's high latex content, several attempts have been made to grow the plant commercially for the production of rubber. The similar appearance of the latex to milk led to a native practice of applying a decoction of dogbane to a mother's breasts to increase lactation. The Blackfoot also used the milky juice as a shampoo to make hair shiny.

bunchberry, pigeonberry

Cornus canadensis L.

WHERE, WHEN AND WHAT TO LOOK FOR

Bunchberry, or pigeonberry, is common to most wooded areas in Alberta. A delicate herb that has been grown in English gardens for over two centuries, it likes cool, shady areas, especially under evergreens, where the soil is quite acidic. Its 'large white flower' appears in **June** and is actually a cluster of 5 to 15 small flowers surrounded by 4 white bracts. Below the 'flower' is a whorl of 4 to 6 oval leaves, each about 8 cm in length. Two smaller, opposite leaves appear on the stem below the whorled leaves. In **August** small, edible, red berries form; they are tasteless to humans but readily eaten by grouse and other birds.

DID YOU KNOW...

The Cree call the bunchberry *kawiscowimin,* meaning 'itchy chin berry', a reference to the rough leaf surface.

red-osier dogwood
Cornus stolonifera Michx.

WHERE, WHEN AND WHAT TO LOOK FOR

Red-osier dogwood is a shrub that inhabits moist riverbanks and wooded areas throughout Alberta. It grows to 3 m and is easily identified by its bright-red bark. Small (1 mm wide) white flowers, 8 to 12 in number, appear from **June through August** in flat-topped clusters, 3 to 6 cm wide. Opposite leaves, 3 to 8 cm long, are dark-green on top and lighter-green underneath; they turn reddish purple in fall. Lower branches sometimes root and form new plants. The berries are juicy, white (sometimes purplish) and 2 to 3 mm in diameter. The berries are inedible because they are very bitter.

DID YOU KNOW…

The Cree and Blackfoot used the bark and leaves of red-osier dogwood as an additive to tobacco. Native peoples from northern Alberta used the outer bark to make a dye and a tanning solution for hides. Snow blindness was treated with an eyewash made from the berries. Stems of red-osier dogwood were woven into birch baskets to add colour.

fireweed,
tall willowherb

Epilobium angustifolium L.

WHERE, WHEN AND WHAT TO LOOK FOR

Fireweed grows in large colonies in open forests, along river banks and in forest-burn areas. It reaches a height of 3 m and has the common name 'fireweed' because it is one of the first plants to appear after a forest fire. Pink to light-purple flowers (2 to 3 cm across) appear in terminal clusters and bloom from **June through August**. Alternate leaves have smooth leaf margins and grow 5 to 20 cm long and up to 3.5 cm wide. The fruit, a pinkish green capsule or pod, is often 4-angled and 4 to 10 cm long. Pods contain many seeds, each with tufts of white hair, 9 to 14 mm long.

DID YOU KNOW...

Young fireweed shoots make an excellent vegetable that tastes like asparagus. The whole plant is readily eaten by livestock, and the flowers are a good source of nectar for bees. The roots and leaves have been used as a remedy for diarrhea, eczema and sore throats.

yellow evening primrose

Oenothera biennis L.

WHERE, WHEN AND WHAT TO lOOK FOR

Yellow evening primrose, a biennial, is common in dry, open areas of southern Alberta. Stems, up to 1.5 m tall, are green with a reddish tinge and have alternate leaves. Flowers, 2 to 5 cm across, consist of 4 sepals that are turned back, 4 bright-yellow petals, 8 stamens and a 4-lobed style. The fruit, a 4-chambered, hairy capsule (2 to 3 cm long), contains numerous seeds.

DID YOU KNOW...

The Blackfoot collected the roots of the yellow evening primrose and dried them as a winter food. Yellow evening primrose is still cultivated in Europe for its root. Young roots taste similar to parsnips; older roots have a peppery flavour. The basal leaves can be collected in the spring and cooked as a pot-herb.

common red paintbrush

Castilleja miniata

Dougl. ex Hook.

yellow paintbrush

WHERE, WHEN AND WHAT TO LOOK FOR

Common red paintbrush can be found in open woods and meadows in the foothills regions of southern Alberta. Plants, up to 60 cm tall, have alternate, stalkless leaves with 3 prominent veins. The red, pink, crimson or yellow petals of the flower are not actually petals but coloured bracts or modified leaves. The flower consists of 4 green, united sepals; 4 green, united petals with some colour at their tips; 4 stamens; and 1 style. The tube-shaped flower is 2 to 3.5 cm long. The fruit, a capsule, contains numerous seeds.

SIMILAR SPECIES

A closely related species, yellow paintbrush, (*C. lutescens* (Greenm.) Rydb.) has yellow bracts that are 3 to 7-lobed. It can be found on grassy slopes in the foothills area.

DID YOU KNOW...

Paintbrush flowers are edible, but should not be eaten in large amounts. **Poisoning is possible** if the plants are growing in soils with a high selenium concentration.

common red paintbrush

elephant head

toadflax, butter-and-eggs
Linaria vulgaris Hill.

WHERE, WHEN AND WHAT TO LOOK FOR

Toadflax, or butter-and-eggs, was introduced to our region from Europe as a garden flower. Now classified as a noxious weed, it is common on roadsides, railway grades, ditches and waste areas. The orange-throated, yellow flower (2 to 3 cm long) has a spur approximately 1 cm long rising from the corolla. Toadflax grows to a height of 60 cm, with alternate leaves up to 7.5 cm long and less than 1 cm wide.

SIMILAR SPECIES

A related species, little red elephant or elephant head (*Pedicularis groenlandica* Retz.), has reddish purple or pinkish flowers that resemble an elephant's head. It is found in wet areas throughout the foothills of southern Alberta.

DID YOU KNOW ...

The common name toadflax originated in England. 'Toad' meant worthless and 'flax' suggests the leaves resemble those of the Flax Family (*Linaceae*). Toadflax spreads by an underground rhizome, making it hard to eradicate in cropland.

toadflax

yellow beard-tongue

Penstemon confertus Dougl.

yellow beard-tongue

WHERE, WHEN AND WHAT TO LOOK FOR

Yellow beard-tongue grows in meadows and open woods of the foothills and mountains of southern Alberta. Slender stems, up to 50 cm tall, have opposite, stalkless leaves 5 to 10 cm long. Pale-yellow flowers, about 1 cm long, appear in interrupted terminal clusters in **June and July**. Flowers have 5 united sepals, 5 united petals (2 upper and 3 lower), 4 stamens and 1 style. The common name beard-tongue refers to a hairy sterile stamen that resembles a tongue. The fruit appears as a capsule that splits lengthwise, releasing numerous, angular seeds.

SIMILAR SPECIES

A closely related species, shrubby beard-tongue (*P. fruticosus* (Pursh) Greene), can be found on dry, mountain slopes. The tube-shaped, lilac-purple flowers are 3.5 to 4.5 cm long.

DID YOU KNOW...

Stems and leaves of yellow beard-tongue can be brewed to make a refreshing tea.

shrubby beard-tongue

smooth blue beard-tongue

Penstemon nitidus Dougl. ex Benth.

WHERE, WHEN AND WHAT TO LOOK FOR

Smooth blue beard-tongue grows in dry, open areas and prairie grassland of southern Alberta. The stout stem grows to a height of 30 cm, with opposite, stalkless leaves, 3 to 5 cm long. The grayish blue leaves are smooth and somewhat fleshy. Blue to purplish, tube-shaped flowers (1.5 to 2 cm long) appear in terminal clusters in **May**. The corolla consists of 2 upper and 3 lower lobes. Also present are 4 stamens and a single, hairy, sterile stamen, called a staminode. The fruit is a many-seeded capsule.

SIMILAR SPECIES

A closely related species, slender blue beard-tongue (*P. procerus* Dougl. ex Grah.) has smaller flowers (6 to 10 mm long) and can be found in meadows and open woodland. Slender blue beard-tongue flowers from **June to August**.

DID YOU KNOW...

Some native peoples treated snakebites with the roots of smooth blue beard-tongue.

39

wild blue flax

Linum lewisii Pursh

yellow flax

WHERE, WHEN AND WHAT TO LOOK FOR

Common in dry, prairie grassland and south-facing slopes, wild blue flax grows throughout Alberta. Its pale-blue flowers (1.5 to 3 cm across) appear from **June through August** and have dark-blue lines radiating from the center. The petals do not survive more than one day. The stem rises from a woody rootstock to a height of 60 cm. Alternate leaves are 1 to 2 cm long, narrow and numerous. The fruit is a dry capsule, 5 mm in diameter, containing 8 to 10 seeds.

SIMILAR SPECIES

A closely related species, yellow flax (*L. rigidum* Pursh), grows on open slopes and prairie grassland. Its yellow flowers, 1 to 1.5 cm across, open at sunrise and close at dusk.

DID YOU KNOW...

The species name *lewisii* comes from the American explorer, Captain Meriwether Lewis, who discovered wild blue flax. The stem fibres of wild blue flax have been used as a substitute for string. The seeds are quite nutritious and contain linseed oil. Early European settlers made a poultice of powdered seeds, corn-meal and boiling water, which they applied to infected wounds.

white geranium

Geranium richardsonii

Fisch. & Trautv.

WHERE, WHEN AND WHAT TO LOOK FOR

The white geranium inhabits edges of aspen and spruce forests in the foothills of southern Alberta. White flowers (up to 3 cm wide) with 5 to 9 distinct, pinkish purple veins bloom from **June through July**. Numerous, bright-green, opposite leaves, 3 to 15 cm broad, have 3 to 7 coarsely serrated lobes. The fruit, a dry capsule with a long beak, splits into 5 parts and releases 5 distinctly veined seeds.

SIMILAR SPECIES

A closely related species, sticky purple geranium (*G. viscosissimum* Fisch. & Mey.), is common in the foothills and mountains of southern Alberta. Its petals are pinkish purple and 14 to 20 mm long. The leaves are 5 to 7-lobed. The entire plant is sticky-hairy.

DID YOU KNOW...

The leaves of the white geranium are edible and can be added to soups and salads. A bath made with geranium leaves is said to stimulate the skin. The Blood people treated headache and colds with the leaves of sticky purple geranium.

salt sage

Atriplex nuttallii S. Wats.

WHERE, WHEN AND WHAT TO LOOK FOR

Salt sage, a perennial sub-shrub, commonly inhabits badlands, eroded slopes and river gravels. The plant, which grows to 60 cm tall, rises from a woody base. Leaves are alternate and opposite, and have a mealy texture. Male plants produce dense terminal clusters of yellow flowers, consisting of 3 to 5 sepals and 3 to 5 stamens. There are no petals. Female plants have greyish green flowers composed of 2 bracts and 1 to 5 styles. There are no sepals or petals. The fruit, an achene, is round and spiny.

DID YOU KNOW...

Salt sage seeds are nutritious and can be ground and mixed with water to make a refreshing beverage. Stems and leaves can be used for stuffing, as a pot-herb or to give a salty flavour to meat. Caution should be exercised when eating this plant. **Poisoning is possible** if the plant is growing in soil with a high selenium concentration. Salt sage is readily eaten by livestock.

grass-of-Parnassus

Parnassia palustris L.

WHERE, WHEN AND WHAT TO LOOK FOR

Grass-of-Parnassus inhabits wet areas in ditches, bogs and shady woods throughout Alberta. Five greenish yellow, sterile stamens (staminodes) make this one of the prettiest flowers in Alberta. The flowers (2.5 cm wide) bloom from **June through September** and are composed of 5 green sepals and 5 white petals with distinct, green veins. The plant grows up to 35 cm tall with 1 or more flowering stems. Basal leaves have smooth leaf margins and are heart-shaped, 1 to 2.5 cm wide. A single stem leaf, located near the midpoint of the flowering stem, makes grass-of-Parnassus easy to identify. The fruit is a dry capsule up to 1 cm long, containing many brown seeds.

SIMILAR SPECIES

Three other species are found in the mountains and foothills of Alberta. Each species has 1 stem leaf. Fringed grass-of-Parnassus (*P. finbriata* Konig), found in moist, springy areas, has frilled petals with 5 distinct veins. Alpine grass-of-Parnassus (*P. kotzebuei* Cham. & Schlecht) is found in moist, alpine slopes and has 3 veins per petal. Small flowered grass-of-Parnassus (*P. parviflora* DC.) is found in boggy areas and has 5 to 7 distinct veins per petal.

harebell

Campanula rotundifolia L.

W H E R E,   W H E N   A N D   W H A T   T O   L O O K   F O R

Harebell inhabits dry hillsides, meadows and the edges of open woods. It grows to 45 cm tall and is found throughout Alberta. Blue, bell-shaped flowers (1.5 to 2.5 cm long) bloom from **June through August**. Flowering stems, each bearing 1 to 5 flowers, rise from the rootstock. Basal leaves are oval; alternate stem leaves are narrow and 1 to 7.5 cm long. The fruit is a papery capsule containing many seeds.

S I M I L A R   S P E C I E S

A closely related species, garden harebell (*C. rapunculoides* L.), has larger flowers and can be found in waste areas where it has escaped from cultivation.

D I D   Y O U   K N O W …

The Cree chopped the dried root of harebell and made it into a compress to stop bleeding, reduce swelling and assist healing. They also chewed the root to relieve heart ailments.

bearberry, kinnikinnick

Arctostaphylos uva-ursi (L.) Spreng.

WHERE, WHEN AND WHAT TO LOOK FOR

Although usually associated with pine forests, bearberry is a low-trailing shrub that can also be found in dry, open areas. A pinkish white, urn-shaped flower (about 5 mm long) appears from **May through July**. Thick, leathery, alternate leaves, 1.5 to 2 cm long, remain green for several seasons. The leaf underside has a network of prominent veins. A bright-red berry, 6 to 10 mm in diameter, appears in August and often remains until the following summer. The dry, tasteless berry contains 5 nutlets.

DID YOU KNOW...

The Vitamin C and carbohydrate content of bearberry make it an important survival food. The red fruit remains on the stems throughout the winter, making it accessible to humans and animals. The acidic berries are said to relieve pain associated with kidney stones. Eating too many of the berries can cause constipation, so they have been used as a treatment for diarrhea. A tea made from bearberry leaves was used as a diuretic and astringent. Early European explorers and trappers dried the leaves and used them as a tobacco substitute.

twining honeysuckle

Lonicera dioica L.

WHERE, WHEN AND WHAT TO LOOK FOR

Twining honeysuckle is a woody vine that climbs on trees, shrubs and fences. It grows in aspen forests throughout Alberta. Young yellow flowers (1.5 to 2.5 cm long) form in clusters inside bowl-shaped, united leaves. Blossoms appear from **July through August** and turn red as they mature. The vine grows up to 2 m and has shredded bark. Opposite, oval leaves, 5 to 8 cm long, are smooth on top, hairy on the underside. Red berries, 5 to 8 mm in diameter, ripen in August.

DID YOU KNOW...

The hollow branches of twining honeysuckle made good stems for corncob pipes. Stems can also serve as drinking straws. An infusion of the inner bark may work as a diuretic.

snowberry

Symphoricarpos albus

(L.) Blake

WHERE, WHEN AND WHAT TO LOOK FOR

An inconspicuous shrub growing in moist, aspen and spruce forests, snowberry is found throughout Alberta. The delicate branches grow up to 50 cm tall. Bell-shaped, pinkish white flowers (4 to 7 mm long) bloom from **June through July**. They appear in clusters of 2 or 3 and are borne in the upper and terminal leaf axils. Opposite, oval leaves (1 to 4 cm long) have soft hairs on the underside. The fruit, a waxy, white berry, is 6 to 12 mm in diameter.

SIMILAR SPECIES

A closely related species, buckbrush (*S. occidentalis* Hook.) has flowers whose stamens are longer than the petals, unlike those in snowberry *(see page 48)*.

DID YOU KNOW...

The juicy, white fruit of snowberry is a strong laxative. The Blackfoot used the plant as a broom.

buckbrush

Symphoricarpos occidentalis

Hook.

WHERE, WHEN AND WHAT TO LOOK FOR

Buckbrush inhabits dry, open areas and the edges of aspen forests. A common shrub in Alberta, buckbrush grows to 1 m tall and forms extensive colonies. Pinkish white flowers (6 mm long) bloom from **June through July**, appearing in clusters at the ends of stems. Its bark is copper-coloured. Oval, opposite leaves are 2 to 6 cm long and greyish green. Whitish green berries, 8 to 10 mm in diameter, appear in August and turn purple as they mature.

DID YOU KNOW ...

Early European settlers called this shrub 'water-brush', believing it grew where the water table was close to the surface. The Blackfoot made arrow shafts from the stems of buckbrush.

low-bush cranberry
Viburnum edule (Michx.) Raf.

WHERE, WHEN AND WHAT TO LOOK FOR

Low-bush cranberry is common in moist, heavily wooded forests in our region. Clusters of 3 to 30 white flowers, each about 7 mm wide, bloom from **June through July**. The shrub grows up to 2 m tall and has greyish brown bark. Opposite leaves (6 to 10 cm long) have 3 indistinct lobes and 3 to 5 prominent veins radiating from the leaf base. Bright-red berries, 1 cm in diameter, contain single seeds and appear from August to September. Usually 2 to 5 berries per cluster reach maturity.

DID YOU KNOW...

The fruit of low-bush cranberry is an excellent source of Vitamin C. The berries are delicious fresh or made into juice or jellies. The tart fruit flavour improves after a frost. The Cree brewed a tea from low-bush cranberry flower buds, twig tips, leaves and stems to relieve sore throats. They also chewed the unopened flower buds and applied them to sores on the lips.

common horsetail

Equisetum arvense L.

reproductive stem

WHERE, WHEN AND WHAT TO LOOK FOR

Common horsetail inhabits moist woods, roadsides, riverbanks and wet meadows throughout Alberta. True flowers (sepals, petals and seeds) are absent. This species has 2 types of stems, each up to 50 cm tall. The brown to pinkish green, fertile stems appear in **early May**. These spore-producing stems have cone-like structures called 'strobili'. These stems wither soon after 'fruiting'. Green, sterile stems appear in late May and produce food for the next year's growth. The sterile stems have whorled branches at each node. Leaves are reduced to 8 to 12 brown, tooth-like scales and are located at the nodes.

DID YOU KNOW...

Horsetails, or scouring-rush as they are sometimes called, have a very high silica content. Scouring-rush got its name from early European settlers, who scrubbed their pots and pans with this plant. It also made a good substitute for sandpaper. Common horsetail was once a valuable commodity because it polished arrows and wooden articles. A wash made from this plant may reduce offensive perspiration, such as foot odour. Horsetails may be poisonous to horses.

vegetative stem

blue-eyed grass
Sisyrinchium montanum Greene

WHERE, WHEN AND WHAT TO LOOK FOR

Blue-eyed grass, a common plant, inhabits moist, open areas. Flowers (1 cm long), bearing 3 blue sepals and 3 blue petals, bloom from **June through July**. Because this plant resembles grass, it is often overlooked when not in flower. It grows up to 30 cm tall, with grass-like basal leaves, 3 mm wide and 2 to 6 cm long, that are set edgewise on the stem. The fruit is a dry, globe-shaped capsule containing numerous, small, black seeds that can be quickly dispersed. The seeds germinate easily in moist, sandy soil.

SIMILAR SPECIES

A closely related species, mountain blue-eyed grass (*S. septentrionale* Bicknell), has narrower leaves and pale, bluish white flowers. It grows in the foothills.

nodding onion

Allium cernuum Roth

WHERE, WHEN AND WHAT TO LOOK FOR

Nodding onion can be found in the foothills of southern Alberta. This plant inhabits prairie slopes and open, aspen forests, rising from a slender bulb to a height of 40 cm. Its nodding, pinkish white flowers (4 to 6 mm long) bloom from **June through July** in clusters of 10 to 20. Each flower bears 3 sepals and 3 petals, all similar in appearance. Numerous basal leaves grow up to 30 cm long. Leaves have the distinct odour of onion and are edible. Fruit appears as a dry capsule with 3 to 6 small black seeds.

DID YOU KNOW ...

All parts of the nodding onion are edible and are said to have medicinal properties. Nodding onion has been used to add flavour to wild game and to aid digestion. Herbalists may prescribe onion for colds and earaches or as an antiseptic for wounds. Nodding onion is also a valuable food source for ground squirrels.

prairie onion
Allium textile Nels. & Macbr.

WHERE, WHEN AND WHAT TO LOOK FOR

Prairie onion, common on dry prairies and hillsides, can be found throughout southern Alberta. The plant rises from a slender bulb to a height of 25 cm. Prairie onion has 2 basal, grass-like leaves, each 1 to 5 mm wide, with the distinct odour of onion. The white to pale-pink flowers appear in umbrella-shaped clusters, called 'umbels', in **May and June**. Flowers consist of 3 sepals and 3 petals, all similar in appearance, 6 stamens and 1 pistil. Fruit appears as a dry capsule containing 6 to 12 small, black seeds.

DID YOU KNOW...

The Blackfoot used the whole prairie onion plant to season meat dishes. The bulbs can be eaten raw or cooked. Prairie onion was also used as a remedy for sore throat.

fairy-bells

Disporum trachycarpum

(S. Wats.) B.& H.

WHERE, WHEN AND WHAT TO LOOK FOR

Fairy-bells grow in moist, aspen forests throughout Alberta. Greenish yellow flowers (1 to 2 cm long) bloom from **May through June**. Flowers bear 3 sepals and 3 petals, all similar in appearance, growing in groups of 1 to 4 at the end of stems. The plant grows to a height of 60 cm. It has drooping branches and dark-green, parallel-veined, alternate leaves up to 7.5 cm long and 5 cm wide. A deep-red berry, 1 cm in diameter with a velvety surface, appears from **July through August** and contains 4 to 18 seeds.

DID YOU KNOW ...

The velvety fruit of fairy-bells can be eaten raw and has a distinct apricot flavour. The Blackfoot called this plant *im-a-toch-kot*, which means 'dog feet'.

western wood lily

Lilium philadelphicum L.

WHERE, WHEN AND WHAT TO LOOK FOR
The western wood lily is occasionally found in the foothills of southern Alberta along roadsides and on the edges of aspen groves. Once quite common, its numbers have been greatly reduced by picking and agricultural expansion. Large, showy, reddish orange flowers bear 3 sepals and 3 petals, all similar in appearance. Below the flower grows a whorl of 4 to 8 leaves, much like the alternate stem leaves, all up to 8 cm in length.

DID YOU KNOW…
Many natives crushed the leaves of the western wood lily to make a poultice for the bite of a small poisonous spider, although we no longer know exactly which species. The Cree ate both the bulbs and the seeds of western wood lily.

false Solomon's-seal

Smilacina racemosa (L.) Desf.

WHERE, WHEN AND WHAT TO LOOK FOR

False Solomon's-seal is found in moist woods in the Cypress Hills and foothills of southern Alberta. Stems are somewhat zig-zagged and up to 1 m tall. The stem bears 5 to 12 alternate, stalkless leaves, 5 to 15 cm long and 4 to 8 cm wide. Numerous, white flowers in an open terminal flower arrangement appear in **June and July**. Flowers, 3 to 6 mm across, bear 3 sepals and 3 petals, all similar in appearance. Stamens are longer than the sepals or petals. The fruit, a reddish purple berry, contains 1 or 2 seeds.

DID YOU KNOW ...

The Blackfoot dried and powdered the starchy, aromatic roots of false Solomon's-seal and applied them to wounds. The Blood people used the leaves in soups and to make hair care products. They used the roots as decorations, to make pickles and to induce abortion. The berries may cause diarrhea if eaten in large quantities.

star-flowered Solomon's-seal
Smilacina stellata (L.) Desf.

WHERE, WHEN AND WHAT TO LOOK FOR

Star-flowered Solomon's-seal, an herb found in moist areas of meadows and open forests, is common throughout our region. A white flower (6 to 10 mm across) blooms in **June**, appearing in terminal clusters of 5 to 12. Each flower bears 3 sepals and 3 petals, all similar in appearance. The stem grows to a height of 70 cm and appears bent. Its 6 to 12 light-green leaves, 2 to 10 cm long, are alternate, although they appear opposite at a casual glance. A purplish green berry with 6 stripes appears from **July through August**.

SIMILAR SPECIES

A closely related species, three-leaved Solomon's-seal (*S. trifolia* (L.) Desf), has 3 leaves and can be found growing in peat bogs and marshes in northern Alberta.

DID YOU KNOW ...

The slender roots of star-flowered Solomon's-seal were gathered and dried in the fall, then ground into a powder and applied to wounds to stop bleeding. Livestock readily eat star-flowered Solomon's-seal.

white camas

Zigadenus elegans Pursh

WHERE, WHEN AND WHAT TO LOOK FOR

White camas can be found in moist meadows and open woods. It grows commonly in the foothills area and occasionally in prairie grassland. The greenish white flowers, up to 2 cm wide, bear 3 sepals and 3 petals, similar in size (7 to 10 mm long) and colour. The plant, up to 60 cm tall, rises from a long, onion-like bulb, with several pale-green, grass-like leaves. Numerous seeds are produced in a dry capsule, 1.5 to 2 cm long.

SIMILAR SPECIES

A closely related species, death camas (*Z. venenosus* S. Wats.), can be found growing alongside white camas. Death camas is **very poisonous** and has resulted in numerous livestock deaths. The creamy-white sepals and petals of death camas are smaller (4 to 5 mm long) than those of white camas.

DID YOU KNOW...

The Blackfoot mashed the bulb of white camas and applied it to swollen or aching legs. No bandage was required because the mash was quite sticky. A mash made from the bulbs of death camas was applied to sprains and bruises.

running club-moss

little club-moss
Selaginella densa Rydb.

WHERE, WHEN AND WHAT TO LOOK FOR

Little club-moss is often overlooked because of its size, colour and resemblance to moss. It is a matted, greyish green perennial of open prairie, sandhills and dry, exposed areas. It is found throughout Alberta. Plants rarely exceed 3 cm in height and are covered in numerous, small (2 to 3 mm long), 1-nerved leaves that have 10 to 24 microscopic hairs on the leaf edge. Leaves appear in whorls of 4 and overlap the ones above. Flowers are absent. Little club-moss reproduces by spores. Spores of 2 types are produced in leaf axils on the 4-sided stems that rise above the mat.

SIMILAR SPECIES

Running club-moss (*Lycopodium annotinum* L.), another prostrate growing, spore producing plant, belongs to the Club-Moss Family (*Lycopodiaceae)* and is found in moist, wooded areas. Running club-moss has leaves that appear in whorls of 6. Spores of one size are borne in a terminal club-shaped structure called a 'strobilus'.

DID YOU KNOW…

The fibrous roots and matted growth habit of little club-moss aid in stopping erosion. The plant has little forage value and thrives in overgrazed pastures.

little club-moss

northern bedstraw

Galium boreale L.

WHERE, WHEN AND WHAT TO LOOK FOR

Northern bedstraw is a common plant in Alberta. It grows in open meadows and at the edges of aspen forests. Fragrant, 4-lobed, white flowers (3 mm across) appear in dense clusters from **June through July**. Square stems grow to a height of 80 cm. Whorled leaves, 2 to 5 cm long with 3 prominent veins, appear in groups of 4. Fruit forms as nutlets, 1 mm in diameter, borne in pairs and covered with dense, white hairs.

DID YOU KNOW...

The common name 'bedstraw' originates from the plant's use as a mattress stuffing by early European settlers. The Cree made a red dye to colour porcupine quills by boiling the roots of bedstraw. Boiled for a longer period of time, the roots produced a yellow dye. Bedstraw belongs to the same family as coffee, and the flavour and aroma of its seeds are said to make it the best coffee substitute of any plant in Canada.

scarlet mallow
Sphaeralcea coccinea
(Pursh) Rydb.

WHERE, WHEN AND WHAT TO LOOK FOR

Scarlet mallow, a perennial herb rarely exceeding 20 cm in height, is common in prairie grassland, roadsides and badlands. It can be found throughout southern Alberta. Leaves are alternate, deeply 3 to 5-lobed and greyish green. Five greyish green sepals (3 to 5 mm long), 5 brick-red petals (10 to 15 mm long), numerous, yellow, united stamens and 1 pistil make up this easily recognized flower. Seeds are produced in 1-seeded segments, similar to hibiscus and hollyhock, well-known ornamental plants of the Mallow Family.

DID YOU KNOW...

The Blackfoot ground scarlet mallow into a paste and applied it to sores and wounds as a cooling agent. This paste was also used by medicine men, who coated their hands and arms with it before reaching into boiling water to demonstrate their supernatural powers.

wild mint

Mentha arvensis L.

WHERE, WHEN AND WHAT TO LOOK FOR

Wild mint grows along the margins of sloughs and in wet, marshy areas. It can be found throughout Alberta. Purplish blue, tube-shaped flowers (3 mm long) appear, clustered in the leaf axils, from **June through August**. Stamens are longer than the 4 or 5-lobed corolla. Greenish purple, square stems grow to 50 cm tall. Opposite leaves, 1 to 4 cm long and 1 to 1.5 cm wide, have the characteristic mint fragrance when crushed. The fruit appears as 4 nutlets enclosed by the sepals.

DID YOU KNOW...

This plant is easily recognized by its distinctive scent. A delicious tea, which has been used to treat colds, can be made from fresh or dried mint leaves and stems. The Blackfoot used the leaves to flavour meat or pemmican. They also boiled snares and traps with the leaves to mask human scent.

marsh
hedge nettle
Stachys palustris L.

WHERE, WHEN AND WHAT TO LOOK FOR

Marsh hedge nettle is commonly found in wet areas throughout
southern Alberta. The plant rises from a creeping rhizome and
is covered in stiff hairs, giving it a light-green appearance. Stems
are square and up to 80 cm tall. Opposite leaves, 2 to 10 cm
long, are stalkless and toothed. Funnel-shaped flowers are borne
in terminal clusters in **July and August**. The 5 united petals (10
to 15 mm long) are mottled white, pink and purple. The fruits
are dark-brown nutlets about 2 mm long.

DID YOU KNOW...

An infusion of marsh hedge nettle leaves was used to wash
sores. The tuberous root of this plant can be eaten boiled,
roasted, raw or dried. Marsh hedge nettle is cultivated for its
root in Asia, where it is often called 'Chinese artichoke'.

wild morning glory
Convolvulus sepium L.

wild buckwheat

WHERE, WHEN AND WHAT TO LOOK FOR

Wild morning glory climbs on shrubs and trees along moist, wooded areas in southern Alberta. It blooms in **June and July**. Its flower (3 to 6 cm across) is a combination of 5 green sepals enclosed by 2 large bracts and 5 white to pinkish, funnel-shaped petals borne in leaf axils. The vine grows to several metres long, with alternate, triangular leaves 5 to 13 cm in length. Fruit appears as a dry capsule containing 4 black seeds that may remain dormant for years until conditions favour germination.

SIMILAR SPECIES

A closely related species, field bindweed (*C. arvensis* L.), has pinkish white flowers (3 to 5 mm long) and smaller leaves (3 to 5 mm long). Field bindweed is often confused with wild buckwheat (*Polygonum convolvulus* L.), a member of the Goosefoot Family. Field bindweed and wild buckwheat both have twining stems, but field bindweed flowers are 2 to 2.5 cm across, while wild buckwheat flowers are less than 0.5 cm across. These weeds were introduced from Europe or Asia and are difficult to eradicate from cultivated fields.

DID YOU KNOW...

Wild morning glory and field bindweed both contain a bitter, milky juice that causes **nausea** if eaten.

wild morning glory

peppergrass
Lepidium densiflorum Schrad.

WHERE, WHEN AND WHAT TO LOOK FOR

Peppergrass inhabits wasteland and dry, open areas throughout Alberta. Its pinkish white flowers (2 to 3.5 mm long) bloom from **June through July**, appearing in racemes 5 to 15 cm long. It grows to a height of 60 cm and has numerous branches, lobed basal leaves and narrow, alternate stem leaves with a few coarse teeth. The heart-shaped fruit (2 to 3 mm wide) has 2 compartments, each containing a single seed.

DID YOU KNOW...

The leaves of peppergrass can be used as a vegetable. They are a good source of potassium, phosphorus, calcium and Vitamins A, B and C. Peppergrass seeds soaked in vinegar can be used as a seasoning for meat. A tea made from peppergrass was sometimes taken to treat kidney problems.

sand bladderpod

Lesquerella arenosa

(Richards.) Rydb.

double bladderpod

WHERE, WHEN AND WHAT TO LOOK FOR

Sand bladderpod is found on dry hillsides, open prairies and gravel flats throughout southern Alberta. The stems of sand bladderpod grow flat along the ground. Leaves, primarily basal, are 1 to 6 cm long and covered in star-shaped hairs. Flowers, 12 mm across, have 4 yellow petals tinged with red or purple. The fruit, a globe-shaped pod called a 'silicle', contains a few brown seeds.

SIMILAR SPECIES

A related species, double bladderpod (*Physaria didymocarpa* (Hook.) A. Gray), has a similar growth habit and grows in dry, open areas of the foothills and mountains. The plant is silvery and has numerous basal leaves. Stem leaves are reduced in size upwards. Yellow flowers appear in **June and July**. The fruit is pod shaped and has 2 inflated lobes, each with 4 seeds.

sand bladderpod

silverberry, wolf willow

Elaeagnus commutata

Bernh. ex Rydb.

WHERE, WHEN AND WHAT TO LOOK FOR

Silverberry, or wolf willow, grows as a shrub. It can be easily identified by its silver coloured leaves. It inhabits edges of aspen stands and overgrazed pastures. Its fragrant flowers are composed of 4 sepals, silver on the outside and yellow on the inside. Petals are absent. Flowers appear in **May to June**, blooming inside leaf axils in clusters of 2 to 5. The purplish brown stem grows to 4 m. Alternate leaves are 2 to 8 cm long and silver on both sides. Silver berries, 1 cm in diameter, have tough skin and a mealy texture. Each berry contains a single seed marked with 8 broad lines.

DID YOU KNOW ...

Native peoples ate silverberry only during food shortages, as the berries are edible but tasteless. They used the bark, cut into strips, as cord or rope and used the dried seeds as beads for necklaces and clothing decorations.

Canada buffalo-berry

Shepherdia canadensis (L.) Nutt.

male flowers

WHERE, WHEN AND WHAT TO LOOK FOR

Common in open woods and on riverbanks, Canada buffalo-berry can be found throughout Alberta. Male and female flowers appear on separate plants and bloom from **May through June**. Flowers have 4 brownish yellow sepals (2 mm across) and no petals. The shrub grows up to 3 m tall, with several stems arising from a single rootstalk. Young shoots are scaly brown; older bark is greyish black. Oblong, opposite leaves appear after the flowers and are 2.5 to 5 cm long, dark-green on top and scaly brown underneath. The red berries, 4 to 6 mm in diameter, form in clusters around the stem.

DID YOU KNOW...

The common name 'buffalo-berry' was used by the Plains peoples. They believed that when the berries were ripe, the buffalo were fat enough to hunt. 'Soapberry' is another common name, because the juice of the berries contains saponin, a substance with a soapy flavour and texture. The fruit was added to buffalo meat for flavouring. It could also be whipped into a dessert called 'Indian ice cream' by European settlers. The flavour of the fruit improves after a frost.

pale coral-root
Corallorhiza trifida Châtelain

WHERE, WHEN AND WHAT TO LOOK FOR

Pale coral-root is a saprophytic herb favouring undisturbed, moist, shaded areas in aspen and spruce forests. Pale, yellowish green flowers appear in **June** and are recognized by their white 'lip', which is often spotted with red or purple. The blooms (5 mm across) grow 3 to 12 per stalk. The greenish yellow stem grows up to 30 cm tall and has a coral-like, branched rhizome and no true roots. Leaves consist of a single basal sheath and several yellowish green scales surrounding the stem. Its dry capsule contains many brown seeds.

SIMILAR SPECIES

There are two other species of coral-root growing in Alberta (spotted coral-root, *C. maculata* Raf., and striped coral-root, *C. striata* Lindl.). These species are not as common as pale coral-root and have larger, striped or spotted flowers and purplish or yellowish brown stems.

DID YOU KNOW ...

The genus name, *Corallorhiza*, refers to the coral-like rhizome of this plant.

yellow lady's-slipper
Cypripedium calceolus L.

sparrow's-egg lady's slipper

WHERE, WHEN AND WHAT TO LOOK FOR

Yellow lady's-slipper grows in moist areas along railway tracks, at the edges of sloughs and peat bogs, and in moist woods and ditches. It is found in Calgary and along the upper Bow River. The pouch-like petal (2 to 4 cm long) is bright-yellow with reddish purple dots. Sepals and remaining petals, greenish brown with purple stripes, are often twisted. Yellow lady's-slipper grows up to 40 cm tall, arising from a stout rhizome and coarse roots. Alternate leaves, 5 to 15 cm long, appear 3 or 4 per stem. The prominently veined leaves are stalkless, pleated and hairy. The fruit appears as a dry capsule with many small brown seeds.

SIMILAR SPECIES

A closely related species, sparrow's-egg lady's-slipper (*C. passerinum* Richards.), is found in wooded areas of the upper Bow River and Kananaskis Country. The 'slipper', 1.5 cm long, is white with purple spots inside.

DID YOU KNOW...

This plant's genus name refers to the slipper of Aphrodite, Greek goddess of love. Aphrodite was believed to have been born on the island of Cyprus; the name *Cypripedium* means 'Cyprus foot'.

yellow lady's slipper

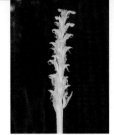

bracted orchid

northern green orchid

Habenaria hyperborea (L.) R.Br.

WHERE, WHEN AND WHAT TO LOOK FOR

Northern green orchid inhabits bogs, wet meadows and moist woods throughout Alberta. It grows up to 60 cm tall, rising from fleshy roots. Its numerous, alternate leaves, 2 to 10 cm long, are parallel veined. The flowers are greenish yellow, about 8 mm wide, and bear 3 sepals and 3 petals. The lower petal, commonly referred to as the 'lip', is longer and wider than the other petals. A slender, pouch-like appendage called a 'spur' (5 mm long) is found at the base of the flower. The fruit appears as a dry capsule with numerous, minute, brown seeds.

SIMILAR SPECIES

A closely related species, bracted orchid (*H. viridis* (L.) R.Br.), is common in moist meadows and woods in the foothills and Rocky Mountains. It is easily distinguished from northern green orchid by its 2 to 3-lobed lip and floral bracts that are longer than the flower.

DID YOU KNOW...

The roots of northern green orchid can be eaten raw or cooked, but should only be collected for food in emergency situations. Orchids are rare and should not be disturbed.

northern green orchid

caragana, Siberian pea tree

Caragana arborescens Lam.

WHERE, WHEN AND WHAT TO LOOK FOR

Introduced from Siberia and Manchuria, the caragana, or Siberian pea tree, is common throughout Alberta. Originally grown for hedges and windbreaks, it has established itself in the natural environment. Bright-yellow flowers (15 to 25 mm long) bloom in **late May**, emerging from scaly buds on slender flower stalks. The shrub grows to a height of 4 m and has greenish brown bark. Alternate, compound leaves, bearing 4 to 6 pairs of oval, spine-tipped leaflets, appear in **May**. The fruit is a narrow pod, 4 to 5 cm long, that turns brown at maturity.

DID YOU KNOW...

In Siberia, farmers feed caragana seeds to their chickens. Farmers also use the young pods as a vegetable.

peavine
Lathyrus ochroleucus Hook.

W H E R E ,   W H E N   A N D   W H A T   T O   L O O K   F O R

Peavine inhabits aspen forests and margins of scrubland throughout our region. Clusters of 5 to 10 yellowish white flowers (each about 1.5 cm long) bloom from **June through July**. A climbing herb, peavine grows to a height of 1 m, grasping onto surrounding vegetation with modified leaf structures called 'tendrils'. Alternate, compound leaves have 3 to 5 pairs of oval leaflets, 2.5 to 5 cm long. The fruit appears as pods up to 4 cm long, containing 4 to 6 seeds that are considered **poisonous** and should not be eaten.

S I M I L A R   S P E C I E S

A closely related species, wild peavine (*L. venosus* Muhl.), has purple flowers and 4 to 6 pairs of leaflets. It is found only in central Alberta.

alfalfa

Medicago sativa L.

WHERE, WHEN AND WHAT TO LOOK FOR

Introduced from southern Europe as a forage crop, alfalfa is now widely distributed throughout Alberta. Dense clusters of 10 to 30 purple to blue (sometimes yellowish white) flowers (7 to 10 mm long) appear in **June**. Alfalfa grows to a height of 90 cm and has a deep taproot, allowing growth in drier areas. Its compound leaves are alternate and have 3 minutely toothed leaflets, 1 to 3 cm long. The fruit is a hairy pod, 6 mm long, coiled 2 to 3 times and containing 8 to 10 yellowish brown seeds.

DID YOU KNOW…

Alfalfa is used as a soil stabilizer to prevent erosion. Like most legumes, alfalfa has the ability to add nitrogen to the soil with the aid of certain bacteria. This process occurs in swollen parts of the roots called 'nodules'.

yellow sweet clover

white sweet clover
Melilotus alba Desr.

WHERE, WHEN AND WHAT TO LOOK FOR

Common in Alberta, white sweet clover grows in roadside ditches and waste areas. It was introduced to our region as a forage crop. Its white flowers (4 mm long) bloom from **June through August**, appearing in dense terminal spikes about 5 to 10 cm long. A biennial, the plant grows from a deep taproot to a height of 2.5 m. The fruit is a smooth pod 3 to 5 mm long, containing 1 to 3 yellowish brown seeds.

SIMILAR SPECIES

A closely related species, yellow sweet clover (*M. officinalis* (L.) Lam.) has yellow flowers and a wrinkled pod.

DID YOU KNOW...

The young leaves and seeds of both species can be added to salads or cooked as a vegetable. When dried, the leaves have a vanilla-like flavour. Bees make excellent honey from sweet clover. This fragrant plant is often added to flower arrangements and sachets. Sweet clovers have also been used in poultices and plasters to relieve rheumatism and other inflammations.

white sweet clover

late yellow loco-weed

Oxytropis monticola A. Gray

WHERE, WHEN AND WHAT TO LOOK FOR

Late yellow loco-weed, can be found in a variety of habitats throughout Alberta. Basal, compound leaves, 6 to 25 cm long, with 17 to 33 leaflets, are silky-hairy, giving the plant a greyish green appearance. Flowering stems, up to 40 cm tall, have 10 to 30 pale-yellow, sometimes bluish, blooms that appear in **June and July**. The papery pods, 15 to 20 mm long, have numerous black and white hairs.

SIMILAR SPECIES

A closely related species, early yellow loco-weed (*O. sericea* Nutt.) has 11 to 17 leaflets and blooms in **May**. Flowers are slightly larger than late yellow loco-weed, and the pods have a leathery texture.

DID YOU KNOW...

Several species of loco-weed grow in Alberta. Many of these species contain a **poisonous** agent that affects the nervous system of animals that ingest them.

showy loco-weed

Oxytropis splendens

Dougl. ex Hook.

WHERE, WHEN AND WHAT TO LOOK FOR

Showy loco-weed can be found in prairie grassland and open woods in the western part of southern Alberta. Basal, compound leaves, 7 to 25 cm long, with 7 to 15 groups of 3 to 4 whorled leaflets, are covered in long, white, silky hairs. The densely-hairy flowering stem can grow up to 35 cm tall and has 12 to 35 blue to reddish purple flowers. The fruit, a papery pod 10 to 17 mm long, is also covered in fine hairs.

SIMILAR SPECIES

A closely related species, reflexed loco-weed, (*O. deflexa* (Pall.) DC.) has blue flowers and grows in similar habitats. It is easily distinguished from showy loco-weed because alternate stem leaves are present. Reflexed loco-weed has compound leaves composed of 15 to 41 leaflets.

DID YOU KNOW...

The Blood people believed that eating loco-weed would treat asthma. They also boiled the plant and applied it to sores.

golden bean

Thermopsis rhombifolia

(Nutt.) Richards.

WHERE, WHEN AND WHAT TO LOOK FOR

Golden bean, or buffalo-bean, can commonly be found in dry, open areas throughout southern Alberta. In Calgary, look for it at Nose Hill Park. Golden-yellow flowers (1 to 2 cm long) bloom from **May to early June**, appearing 10 to 20 per cluster. The plant grows up to 50 cm tall, often in large patches. Alternate, compound leaves have 3 oval leaflets, 2 to 4 cm long. The fruit is a brown, curved or twisted pod, 3 to 7 cm long, covered with numerous grey hairs and containing 5 to 13 seeds.

DID YOU KNOW...

The flowering of the golden bean indicated to the Blood people that the buffalo were fat enough to kill, hence its other common name 'buffalo-bean'. Some natives made a dye from the flowers of golden bean to colour skin bags and arrows. All parts of the golden bean plant are **poisonous** and cause respiratory paralysis.

white clover, Dutch clover

Trifolium repens L.

red clover

WHERE, WHEN AND WHAT TO LOOK FOR

White, or Dutch, clover was introduced to our region from Europe in the early 1900s as a forage crop, but is now common in gardens, lawns, waste areas and roadsides. Its 15 to 20 whitish pink flowers (8 mm long) appear on short stalks in globe-shaped clusters 1 to 2 cm in diameter. The compound leaves are composed of 3 leaflets, each about 2 cm in length. The plant's scientific name refers to its 'three leaves' (*Trifolium*) and 'creeping nature' (*repens*). Fruits appear from **June through August** as pods 8 mm in length, containing 2 to 5 seeds.

SIMILAR SPECIES

A closely related species, red clover (*T. pratense* L.), has pink flowers (12 to 20 mm long) that appear in larger clusters, 2 to 5 cm in diameter. Its leaves are somewhat hairy, and its pods are yellow to purple and single-seeded.

DID YOU KNOW...

Young white clover leaves contain large amounts of Vitamins A, B, D, E, K, as well as some minerals. They make an tasty addition to soups, salads and cereals, but only in small quantities because they are difficult to digest. Dried flowers and seeds were used for breadmaking in times of famine.

white clover

wild vetch

Vicia americana Muhl.

WHERE, WHEN AND WHAT TO LOOK FOR

Wild vetch, a climbing herb that grows to 40 cm long, grasps onto surrounding vegetation with tendrils. It inhabits open grasslands and the edges of aspen forests and can be found throughout our region. Clusters of 3 to 9 purple to reddish purple flowers (each 1.5 to 2 cm long) bloom from **June through July**. Compound leaves are alternate with 8 to 14 oval leaflets, each 1.5 to 3.5 cm long and prominently veined. The pods, 2.5 to 3 cm long, contain 4 to 7 seeds.

DID YOU KNOW...

Wild vetch seeds can be added to soups and salads. Dried seeds can be used as a replacement for caraway. Young stems can be baked or cooked as a pot-herb. Caution should be exercised when using wild vetch, as some sources indicate the seeds may be **poisonous**.

moss phlox

moss phlox
Phlox hoodii Richards.

WHERE, WHEN AND WHAT TO LOOK FOR

Moss phlox can be commonly found on dry, eroded slopes and prairie grassland throughout southern Alberta. This semi-woody plant is inconspicuous when not in bloom. Stems rarely exceeding 3 cm, blend in with the surrounding vegetation. Leaves are opposite, awl-shaped, 5 to 7 mm long and covered in fine hairs. Tube-shaped flowers, 1 cm across with 5 lobes, are white to pale-blue and appear at the end of branches. Flowers bloom in **early May**. The fruit, a capsule, contains few seeds.

SIMILAR SPECIES

A related species, narrow-leaved collomia (*Collomia linearis* Nutt.), grows to 45 cm and has alternate leaves 2 to 4 cm long. Trumpet-shaped, pink flowers are borne in terminal clusters from **June to September**.

DID YOU KNOW...

Some reports indicate the Blood people used the flowers of moss phlox to produce a dye.

narrow-leaved collomia

white spruce
Picea glauca (Moench) Voss

WHERE, WHEN AND WHAT TO LOOK FOR

White spruce is common in the foothills and Cypress Hills of southern Alberta. It grows up to 40 m tall in a variety of soils and habitats. The needle-shaped leaves, less than 1.5 cm in length, appear 4-sided in cross-section and do not fall for several years. Its drooping cones are 2.5 to 5 cm long and brown; the cones have rigid seed scales. Seeds are dispersed in autumn, and the cones fall off during the winter.

SIMILAR SPECIES

A closely related species, Engelmann spruce (*P. engelmannii* Parry ex Engelm.), is common at subalpine elevations of the Rocky Mountains. It grows to 30 m tall. Needles grow more than 1.5 cm long and are not sharp-pointed like those of white spruce. The cones have flexible scales and are 3 to 8 cm long.

DID YOU KNOW...

The Cree sewed birch baskets with small spruce roots. They made canoe paddles, fishnet floats and canoe ribs from spruce wood. Spruce sap can be chewed as gum and was used as a sealant for birch bark canoes. The inner bark of white spruce is said to reduce thirst, clean teeth and serve as an emergency food source. Needles and young twigs can be brewed as a tea.

Pursh's plantain

Plantago patagonica Jacq.

WHERE, WHEN AND WHAT TO LOOK FOR

Pursh's plantain thrives on dry plains and eroded slopes of southern Alberta. The plant is silky-woolly throughout. Basal leaves, 3 to 10 cm long and less than 1 cm wide, have 1 to 3 prominent nerves on the leaf underside. The flowering stalk, up to 20 cm tall, has numerous, small, white flowers, 3 to 5 mm wide. Flowers have 4 united sepals, 4 united petals, 4 stamens and 1 style. Sepals and petals are white and papery. The fruit, a capsule, contains 2 small, brown seeds.

SIMILAR SPECIES

A closely related species, common plantain (*P. major* L.), grows as a weed in waste areas, roadsides and lawns. Its glabrous leaves are broad and have 3 to 7 prominent veins.

DID YOU KNOW...

The native name for Pursh's plantain means 'herb to make a hat', referring to the plant's woolly leaves.

fairy candelabra

Androsace septentrionalis L.

WHERE, WHEN AND WHAT TO LOOK FOR

Fairy candelabra, or pygmy-flower, commonly found in dry, open areas of Alberta, is often overlooked because of its size. It grows at elevations ranging from prairie grassland to alpine meadows. Plants can reach 15 cm and have several flowering stems. Leaves are all basal, 5 to 25 mm long, and have smooth or toothed edges. Up to 40 small, white, cup-shaped flowers borne on slender stems appear from **May to August**. The fruit is a many-seeded capsule with five compartments.

SIMILAR SPECIES

A closely related species, sweet-flowered androsace or rock jasmine (*A. chamaejasme* Host), is a small, tufted perennial of mountain slopes. The plant is densely hairy and has larger, cream-coloured flowers with a yellow or pink center.

DID YOU KNOW...

Pygmy-flower is an annual or winter annual that thrives on cultivated land. Populations have increased over the past few years due to changes in agricultural practices.

saline shooting-star

Dodecatheon pulchellum
(Raf.) Merr.

WHERE, WHEN AND WHAT TO LOOK FOR

Shooting-star grows in wet areas, calcareous bogs and saline sloughs. It is common in central and southern Alberta. Flowers bloom in **late June**, appearing in numbers of 3 to 20 on flowering stems 5 to 50 cm tall. The flowers are composed of 5 pink to purple petals curved backwards and 5 bright-yellow, fused stamens, giving the plant its striking colour contrast. Light-green, somewhat fleshy, basal leaves are spatulate and 4 to 17 cm long. The dry capsule splits into 5 sections, each containing numerous seeds 2 to 3 mm long.

SIMILAR SPECIES

A closely related species, mountain shooting-star (*D. conjugens* Greene) is found in drier habitats at higher elevations.

DID YOU KNOW...

The genus name of this plant is Greek for 'twelve gods', the number of gods on Mount Olympus.

mealy primrose

Primula incana M.E. Jones

Mealy primrose appears at the edges of sloughs, calcareous bogs and saline meadows. It can be found in the upper Bow River, Cypress Hills and Drumheller area. Flowers (6 to 10 mm across) are pale-lilac to pink with 5 petals so deeply notched they look like 10. Flowers appear in **late June**. The stem reaches a height of 30 cm and is covered in a mealy, white powder. Basal leaves, 2 to 6 cm long, are light-green on top and powdery-white underneath. The fruit is a capsule containing many seeds, 0.5 to 0.7 mm in diameter.

SIMILAR SPECIES

A closely related species, dwarf Canadian primrose (*P. mistassinica* Michx.), has been found in the upper Bow valley. A rare plant in Alberta, it grows in marshy areas of the mountains.

saskatoon, service-berry

Amelanchier alnifolia Nutt.

WHERE, WHEN AND WHAT TO LOOK FOR

Saskatoon grows at the edges of aspen forests and in dry, open areas throughout Alberta. White flowers bear 5 petals (9 to 20 mm long) appear from **May through June** and are borne in dense terminal clusters at the ends of the branches. The shrub grows up to 4.5 m and has rough, greyish brown bark and alternate, oval leaves, 1 to 5 cm in length. Delicious, dark-purple berries, up to 1 cm in diameter, appear in July.

DID YOU KNOW...

The nutritional value of the saskatoon has been known for centuries. The fruit contains a high concentration of iron and copper. Native peoples and European settlers used the plant as an important staple food. The Blackfoot mixed buffalo fat, blood and saskatoon berries and ate this as a favourite dessert. The berries were a major ingredient in pemmican and were also used to make a purple dye. The Blood people ground saskatoon roots to make a tobacco substitute.

round-leaved hawthorn

Crataegus rotundifolia Moench

WHERE, WHEN AND WHAT TO LOOK FOR

Round-leaved hawthorn grows on south-facing slopes of river valleys and coulees. It tends to grow beside thorny buffalo-berry (*Shepherdia argentea* Nutt.) and chokecherry (*Prunus virginiana* L.). Clusters of 6 to 15 flowers (10 to 15 mm across) appear from **May through June**. The shrub grows up to 5 m tall, bearing stout thorns 2 to 7 cm long. Alternate leaves are 2 to 7 cm long, round, with doubly serrated margins and shallow lobes. The red, berry-like fruit is 1 cm across and has several seeds and little pulp.

DID YOU KNOW...

The fruit of hawthorn is high in sugar, low in fat and protein, but may be **toxic** if consumed in large quantities. Native peoples ate boiled hawthorn berries as a treatment for constipation, and they prepared a hawthorn tea as a stimulant. They made probes, awls and fish hooks from the sharp spines, and digging sticks and clubs from the hard wood.

yellow dryad

yellow dryad, mountain avens

Dryas drummondii Richards.

WHERE, WHEN AND WHAT TO LOOK FOR

Mountain avens, a low-growing, prostrate shrub, forms dense, matted colonies on gravel slopes, river banks and roadsides. It can be found in the foothills and Rocky Mountains of southern Alberta. Older branches are woody and root freely in the soil; young branches are covered in white, woolly hairs. Alternate leaves, 1 to 3 cm long, are dark-green above and woolly-white below. Flowering stalks, up to 25 cm tall, bear a single flower consisting of 8 sepals, 8 yellow petals and numerous stamens and styles. Flowers appear in **June and early July**. The feathery styles elongate as the fruit matures. The styles usually twist together when the fruit is immature or during rainy weather. Dense carpets of fruits, with feathery styles, can be seen by **mid-August**.

SIMILAR SPECIES

A closely related species, white dryad (*D. octopetala* L.), has 8 white petals. It is a common shrub of alpine meadows.

DID YOU KNOW...

The leaves of mountain avens can be used to make tea.

white dryad

yellow avens

Geum aleppicum Jacq.

WHERE, WHEN AND WHAT TO LOOK FOR

Yellow avens, a rough-textured plant of moist woods and meadows, can be found throughout Alberta. The stems, up to 1 m tall, have numerous basal leaves consisting of 5 to 7 toothed leaflets. The alternate stem leaves, composed of 3 to 5 leaflets, are stalkless and reduced in size upwards. Bright-yellow flowers, 10 to 25 mm across, appear in **June and July**. A cluster of achenes, about 1 cm in diameter, appears in late summer. Each achene has a hooked beak that attaches easily to clothing or fur to disperse the fruit.

SIMILAR SPECIES

A closely related species, also called yellow avens (*G. macrophyllum* Willd.), can be distinguished from the previous species by a large terminal leaflet that is not 3-lobed. It is usually found in the foothills of southern Alberta.

DID YOU KNOW...

The whole yellow avens plant can be cooked as a pot-herb.

old man's whiskers, prairie smoke

Geum triflorum Pursh

WHERE, WHEN AND WHAT TO LOOK FOR

Three-flowered avens or torchflower, other common names for this plant, can be found in dry, open areas of southern Alberta. Stems grow up to 40 cm tall and have several basal leaves and 1 or 2 stem leaves. These hairy leaves have 9 to 19 leaflets, each with several lobes or toothed segments. The black rootstalk often retains old leaf stalks from previous years. Flowering stalks usually have 3 nodding flowers, 12 to 20 mm across, and appear in **May and June**. Flowers consist of 5 purplish pink sepals, 5 yellow or pink petals and numerous stamens and pistils. The feathery styles stand erect and elongate as the fruit matures. Carpets of these plants, with their feathery styles blowing in the wind, resemble smoke from a prairie fire.

DID YOU KNOW ...

From the roots and fruits of old man's whiskers, the Blackfoot made an extract that they used as an eyewash. The Blood people used the roots to treat sore gums or eyes, snowblindness, saddle sores and diarrhea. The roots were brewed with fat as a treatment for chapped lips and chicken pox.

shrubby cinquefoil
Potentilla fruticosa L.

snow cinquefoil

WHERE, WHEN AND WHAT TO LOOK FOR

Shrubby cinquefoil grows in the plains and open woods of
southern Alberta, from prairie to sub-alpine elevations. It is also
often grown as an ornamental in yards and gardens. Stems, up
to 150 cm tall, have alternate, compound leaves with 5 to 7
leathery leaflets. The flowers, 25 mm across, are composed of 5
green sepals, 5 yellow petals and numerous stamens and styles.
They appear at the ends of branches in **June to August**. The
fruit is a cluster of achenes.

SIMILAR SPECIES

A closely related species, snow cinquefoil (*P. nivea* L.),
commonly found in alpine meadows, rarely exceeds 15 cm in
height. The plant is densely woolly throughout.

DID YOU KNOW ...

The dried leaves of shrubby cinquefoil make a gold-coloured tea
that has a high calcium content. Some herbalists believe the
powdered roots can be used as a poultice for mouth and skin sores.

shrubby cinquefoil

chokecherry

Prunus virginiana L.

WHERE, WHEN AND WHAT TO LOOK FOR

Chokecherry grows throughout Alberta at the edges of aspen forests and in dry, open areas. Dense, cylindrical clusters of up to 35 white flowers (each 1 to 1.5 cm across) bloom from **May through June**. The shrub grows to a height of 5 m and has greyish brown bark. Alternate leaves are 2 to 8 cm long, with finely serrated margins. Fruit appears as a small purple to black cherry, 6 to 8 mm across.

DID YOU KNOW...

Although sour to the taste, chokecherries make delicious jams and jellies. The Blackfoot ground the entire fruit (including the pit, although it is **slightly toxic**) and formed it into dry cakes which they ate as trail food. They added ground chokecherries to pemmican and fish. The Blood people boiled the fruit with blood as a treat. A strong, black tea made from the fruit was used to treat coughs and colds. The Cree boiled chokecherry twigs to make a tonic to relieve fever. All parts of the chokecherry, except the fruit, may contain hydrocyanic acid and may be **poisonous** if consumed.

prickly rose
Rosa acicularis Lindl.

WHERE, WHEN AND WHAT TO LOOK FOR

Prickly rose, the floral emblem of Alberta, is a prickly stemmed shrub inhabiting woods, roadsides and pastures. It is found throughout the province. Flowers (5 to 8 cm across) appear from **June through July**. Flowers are deep-pink to pale-rose with numerous yellow stamens in their centres. Prickly rose grows to a height of 1.5 m. Alternate, compound leaves have 3 to 7 oval, coarsely toothed leaflets. The red fruit, called a 'hip', is round to pear-shaped and contains several hairy fruits.

SIMILAR SPECIES

A closely related species, the Woods' rose (*R. woodsii* Lindl.), has a globe-shaped fruit and 5 to 9 leaflets. It has fewer thorns than the prickly rose. The two species are known to hybridize.

DID YOU KNOW ...

The rose hip has a high Vitamin C content. Teas, jams and jellies can be made from the petals and hips of these plants. Native peoples placed rose branches around the home of a deceased person to prevent the ghost from returning and haunting the home. Relatives of the deceased person also drank a tea made from the branches to protect themselves.

red raspberry
Rubus idaeus L.

WHERE, WHEN AND WHAT TO LOOK FOR

Red raspberry is common throughout Alberta. It grows in open, aspen forests, burned-over areas, riverbanks and roadside ditches. White flowers (8 to 15 mm across) appear in terminal clusters in **early June**. A red berry, 1 cm across, ripens in July. The shrub grows to a height of 2 m with bristly, reddish-brown stems, some of which survive more than two years. Alternate, compound leaves have 3 to 5 oval, crinkled leaflets, each 5 to 10 cm long.

DID YOU KNOW...

A tea made from the berries and leaves of this well-known plant is said by some to relieve morning sickness when taken during pregnancy. Warm tea taken during labour is said to have a relaxing effect. A poultice prepared from the leaves and fruit was used to soothe wounds, burns and insect bites. Raspberries are delicious fresh; if picked in large quantities, they can be made into jams and wine.

bastard toad-flax

Comandra umbellata

(L.) Nutt.

Geocaulon lividum

WHERE, WHEN AND WHAT TO LOOK FOR

Bastard toadflax commonly grows in prairie grassland, dry, open areas and gravel slopes throughout Alberta. This semi-parasitic plant attaches its roots to those of other plants with small, sucker-like organs. The plant produces its own food but takes water from its host. Toadflax, which grows up to 30 cm tall, has numerous, alternate, stalkless leaves, each up to 25 mm long. Flowers consist of 5 greenish white sepals, each about 5 mm long and united to form a tube. There are no petals. Flowers form a dome-shaped cluster at the top of the stem. The fruit is a dry, 1-seeded drupe containing a single seed.

SIMILAR SPECIES

A related species, also called bastard toad-flax (*Geocaulon lividum* (Richards.) Fern.), is somewhat parasitic on the roots of spruce. It can be found in moist, mossy areas of the upper Bow Valley. In **June**, 3 greenish bronze flowers appear in the leaf axils, giving way to a round, scarlet-coloured berry in late **August**.

DID YOU KNOW...

The fruit of bastard toadflax can be eaten raw. Eating large amounts of fruit may cause nausea.

Comandra umbellata

leafy spurge, wolf's milk

Euphorbia esula L.

WHERE, WHEN AND WHAT TO LOOK FOR

Leafy spurge, or wolf's milk, is a deep-rooted perennial that grows as a weed in sandy roadside ditches and waste areas and on cultivated land. It is found throughout Alberta. Greenish yellow flowers appear in **late June**. Flower clusters have 4 crescent-shaped glands and are borne in 2 leaf-like bracts, 1 cm wide and 1.2 cm long. Male flowers have a single stamen; female flowers have a single pistil. Sepals and petals are absent. The greenish yellow plant grows up to 90 cm tall and has alternate leaves, 2 to 7.5 cm long. The leaves below the flower often appear whorled. The fruit is a capsule, 3 mm long, which bursts open when ripe to release 3 seeds.

DID YOU KNOW...

Leafy spurge is a weed introduced from Europe and Asia. The milky juice of leafy spurge irritates sensitive skin and the digestive tract. This plant may be **toxic** and is not recommended for consumption. Legend says that the plant supplies the devil with milk.

common stonecrop

Sedum lanceolatum Torr.

WHERE, WHEN AND WHAT TO LOOK FOR

Common stonecrop grows on dry slopes and rocky outcrops of the foothills and mountains of southern Alberta. It is also found in the Cypress Hills. A mat-forming plant, common stonecrop has 2 types of stems: sterile and flowering. The sterile stems have numerous leaves and no flowers. The succulent, reddish, flowering stems, up to 15 cm tall, have fleshy, alternate leaves (3 to 15 mm long) that look round in cross-section. The leaves act as water-storage devices, enabling the plant to survive long periods of drought. Flowers, up to 1 cm across, appear in dense terminal clusters in **June to August**. Flowers consist of 4 or 5 greenish yellow sepals, 4 or 5 bright-yellow petals, 8 to 10 stamens and 4 or 5 styles. The pod-like fruits appear in a cluster of 4 or 5.

DID YOU KNOW...

In China, stonecrops are planted in pots and placed on the roofs of houses. The plant is believed to ward off famine and house fires. Stonecrop leaves have a high Vitamin C content, but should be eaten in moderation as they may cause **allergic reactions**.

western Canada violet
Viola canadensis L.

WHERE, WHEN AND WHAT TO LOOK FOR

The western Canada violet grows in moist aspen woods and occasionally under spruce. Flowers (1 to 2.5 cm across) bloom from **June through August**, each appearing as 5 white petals with purplish veins and a yellow throat. The plant grows up to 60 cm tall, often forming large colonies from an underground root system. Alternate leaves are heart shaped, up to 10 cm across and larger at the bottom of the stem than at the top. The fruit is a dry capsule 8 to 12 mm long with several short spines.

DID YOU KNOW...

Western Canada violet is prescribed by some herbalists for the relief of pain associated with cancer. Violet tea is a remedy for stomach and bowel complaints. The Blood people collected the flowers of a closely related species, the early blue violet (*V. adunca* J.E. Smith), to make a dye for colouring arrows.

balsam poplar

Populus balsamifera L.

male catkin

WHERE, WHEN AND WHAT TO LOOK FOR

Balsam poplar grows in moist areas in river valleys. Male catkins are red; females are greyish white and borne on separate trees in **late April**, before the leaves. The alternate leaves are 8 to 15 cm long and have a shiny upper surface. The tree grows to 25 m, with deeply furrowed bark. Sticky buds enclose the young leaves; these buds can be a nuisance in the spring, sticking to shoes, cars and pets. Small, green capsules containing small seeds and cottony hairs ripen in **June**.

DID YOU KNOW ...

The sap of all species of the Willow Family contains a chemical called salicin, which is chemically related to aspirin. The Blackfoot made a tonic from balsam poplar sap to reduce fever and headaches. They used an extract from the buds of balsam poplar to treat snow blindness and to make perfume. They also made a poultice from fresh balsam poplar leaves to apply to sores. The primary method of reproduction in most poplar species is root suckering.

leaf and bark

western cottonwood

Populus deltoides Marsh.

WHERE, WHEN AND WHAT TO LOOK FOR

Western cottonwood is commonly found on riverbanks and moist, sandy areas of southern Alberta. Trees can reach 25 m under favourable conditions. The bark of mature specimens is usually grey and deeply furrowed. Catkins appear in **April** before the leaves emerge. Male flowers may have as many as 60 stamens per flower. Female catkins produce several capsules, 6 to 10 mm long, that release a cottony mass of seeds in **June**. Alternate, triangular leaves, 5 to 10 cm long, have coarsely-toothed or wavy margins. The leaf stalk is flat, which allows the leaf to move even in light breezes.

DID YOU KNOW…

Plains peoples ate the inner bark of the western cottonwood. Leaf buds, catkins and seeds can be eaten raw or in stews. Leaf buds were also boiled to make a yellow dye that was applied to feathers and arrows.

trembling aspen, white poplar

Populus tremuloides Michx.

male catkin

WHERE, WHEN AND WHAT TO LOOK FOR

Trembling aspen, or white poplar, is the most common tree in Alberta. Greyish white male catkins (2 to 4 cm long) and female catkins (4 to 10 cm long) are borne on separate trees in **late April**, before the leaves appear. Alternate, oval leaves are 4 to 7 cm long, with a dark-green upper surface and a pale underside. The flattened petiole allows the leaf to move even in the slightest breeze, hence the name 'trembling' aspen. The tree grows up to 20 m tall, with a trunk up to 60 cm in diameter. Bark is greenish white in younger trees, becoming furrowed with age. Fruit appears as small, green capsules that split when mature. The seeds are covered in a cottony mass commonly seen in June and July.

DID YOU KNOW...

The white, powdery substance found on the trunks of trembling aspen can be used to stop cuts from bleeding. Fresh leaves can be crushed and applied directly to bee stings to reduce irritation. The dry, rotten wood of aspen was used to smoke whitefish and moose meat.

pink wintergreen

Pyrola asarifolia L.

WHERE, WHEN AND WHAT TO LOOK FOR

Pink wintergreen, common in aspen forests, is found throughout Alberta. Nodding, pink flowers (1 to 2 cm across) appear 5 to 15 per stalk and are easily recognized by their long, protruding styles. Flowering stalks often remain into the following summer. The plant grows up to 30 cm tall, often in small patches. The basal leaves are leathery (2 to 7 cm across) and remain green and shiny throughout the winter. Fruit appears as a dry capsule which releases many seeds in **late August**.

DID YOU KNOW ...

Early botanists thought the leaves of pink wintergreen resembled those of wild ginger, hence the Latin name *asarifolia,* meaning 'leaves that look like wild ginger'. Mashed leaves applied to an insect bite may relieve pain and swelling. An infusion of the leaves has been used to treat sore eyes.

greenish-flowered wintergreen

Pyrola chlorantha Sw.

one-flowered wintergreen

WHERE, WHEN AND WHAT TO LOOK FOR

Greenish-flowered wintergreen commonly grows in moist forests in the foothills of southern Alberta. Leaves are basal, leathery, round and 1 to 3 cm wide. Flowering stems, up to 20 cm tall, have 3 to 10 greenish white flowers, 8 to 15 mm across, consisting of 5 sepals (1 to 1.5 mm long), 5 petals (4 to 7 mm long), 10 stamens and a style that curves upward. Seeds are produced in a capsule that splits lengthwise to release them.

SIMILAR SPECIES

A related species, one-flowered wintergreen (*Moneses uniflora* (L.) A. Gray), has a single white flower per stem. It is often found growing in the same habitat as greenish-flowered wintergreen.

DID YOU KNOW...

The leaves of greenish-flowered wintergreen remain green under the snow and can be used as an emergency food source.

greenish-flowered wintergreen

Glossary

ACHENE

Dry, one-seeded fruit that does not open when ripe.

ANNUAL

Plant whose life cycle is completed in one growing season.

ANTHER

The portion of the stamen that produces pollen.

APEX

Tip of a leaf or petal.

AXIL

The angle formed between the leaf and the stem.

BASAL

At or towards the base of the structure

BIENNIAL

A plant that germinates one year, produces seeds the following year, then dies.

BRACT

Leaf-like structure found below a flower or flower cluster.

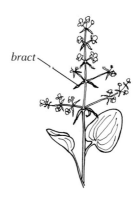

bract

CALCAREOUS

Soils with a high calcium content.

CALYX

Structure formed by the union of the sepals.

CAPSULE

A dry fruit that opens when mature.

CATKIN

Type of flowering stalk on which male or female flowers lack petals.

CLEFT
Deeply lobed.

COMPOUND LEAF
A leaf composed of two or more leaflets.

CONIFEROUS
Cone-bearing plants.

COROLLA
Structure formed by the union of the petals.

DECIDUOUS
Having leaves that fall in autumn.

DECOCTING
A process by which substances are extracted by boiling.

DISC FLORET
Small flowers, usually tube-shaped, in the Aster Family. *(See ray floret.)*

DRUPELET
One part of an aggregate fruit, like those of raspberries.

EMERGENT
A plant whose stem rises out of the water.

FIBROUS
Thread-like roots of plants.

FRUIT
The part of the plant that contains seeds.

GENUS
(PL. GENERA)
A group of species having similar characteristics.

GLABROUS
Without hair.

GLAND
A structure that usually produces nectar or another sticky substance.

HERB
A plant having no woody stems.

INVOLUCRE
A bract or group of bracts below a flower cluster.

involucre

NODE

The point at which the leaf is attached to the stem.

NOXIOUS

A plant that may compete with agricultural crops.

NUTLET

A small nut.

OVARY

Part of the pistil containing the ovules.

OVATE

Egg-shaped and broader at the base, usually in reference to leaves.

OVULE

Undeveloped seeds, contained in the ovary.

PAPPUS

Hairs or bristles that are attached to the fruit in the Aster Family.

PARASITE

A plant that obtains food and nutrients from another living plant.

PERENNIAL

A plant, or part of a plant, living more than two growing seasons.

PETAL

An interior, modified flower leaf, often brightly coloured.

PETIOLE

The stalk of a leaf.

PINNATE

Compound leaf with leaflets arranged on both side of the stalk. *(See illustration, page xiii.)*

PISTIL

The female part of the flower, normally composed of the ovary, style and stigma.

POD

A dry fruit that releases its seeds when mature.

POLLEN

The male spores of plants, usually resembling dust.

POULTICE

A moist mass of herbs applied to the body as external medicine.

PRICKLE

A spiny structure on the surface of a plant.

RACEME
Flower cluster with flowers that bloom up from the bottom of the cluster.

RAY FLORET
Strap-like, often marginal flower type in the Aster Family.

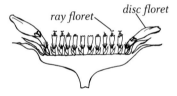

ray floret — *disc floret*

RHIZOME
An elongated, underground stem.

ROSETTE
A cluster of basal leaves.

SAMARA
A dry fruit having wing-like structures.

SAPROPHYTE
A plant that obtains food and nutrients from decaying material.

SEMI-AQUATIC
A plant capable of living in water and on wet shorelines.

SEPALS
The outermost part of the flower; usually green and leaf-like.

SERRATED
Leaf margin having jagged edges.

SHEATH
The base of the leaf that surrounds the stem.

SHRUB
Woody plant having many stems arising from the root.

SIMPLE LEAF
A leaf with a single blade.

S P A T H E

A large bract which encloses a flower cluster.

S P A T U L A T E

Spoon-shaped.

S P E C I E S

A group of similar plants capable of interbreeding to produce offspring like themselves.

S P O R E

An asexual reproductive structure in ferns and fern allies.

S P U R

A slender projection from the corolla or calyx.

S T A L K

A stem; any supporting organ (eg. petiole).

S T A M E N

The male part of the flower, usually composed of an anther and a filament (stalk).

S T A M I N O D E

A sterile stamen.

S T E R I L E

A flower without functional reproductive structures.

S T I G M A

The female receptive surface that pollen grains attach to.

S T Y L E

The elongated part of the pistil between the stigma and the ovary.

S U C K E R

A shoot that grows from the underground part of the plant.

T A P R O O T

The main root, like those of carrots.

T E N D R I L

A clasping or twining part of a leaf.

T E R M I N A L

The end of the stem or leaf.

T H A L L U S

A plant without differentiation between stems and leaves.

TREE

A woody plant having one stem arising from the root.

TRUE FLOWER

Flower possessing stamens and/or pistils.

UMBEL

Flower arrangement where the flower stalks originate from one point.

VASCULAR TISSUE

Specialized conductive vessels in plants, used in transportation of food and water.

Bibliography

Alberta Agriculture. 1983. *Weeds of Alberta*. Alberta Agriculture and Alberta Environmental Centre, Edmonton, Alberta.

Angier, Bradford. 1978. *Field Guide to Medicinal Wild Plants*. Stackpole Books, Harrisburg, Pennsylvania.

Angier, Bradford. 1974. *Guide to the Edible Wild Plants*. Stackpole Books, Harrisburg, Pennsylvania.

Brown, Annora. 1970. *Old Man's Garden*. Gray's Publishing, British Columbia.

Burgess, Jean. 1980. *Walk on the Wild Side: An All Season Trail Guide to Elk Island National Park*. Friends of Elk Island Society, Fort Saskatchewan, Alberta.

Elliott, Douglas B. 1976. *Roots, An Underground Botany and Forager's Guide*. Chatam Press, Old Grenwich, Connecticut.

Fielder, Mildred. 1975. *Plant Medicine and Folklore*. Winchester Press, New York.

Forestry Branch. 1980. *Guide to Forest Understory Vegetation in Saskatchewan, Technical Bulletin No. 9*. Saskatchewan Tourism and Renewable Resources, Regina, Saskatchewan.

Gibbons, Euell. 1966. *Stalking the Healthful Herbs*. Alan C. Hood & Co. Inc., Pitney, Vermont.

Gleason, Henry A. 1963. *The New Britton and Brown Illustrated Flora of the Northeastern United States and Adjacent Canada*. Hafner Publishing Company, Inc., New York and London.

Jackson, Stephen, and Linda Prine. 1978. *Wild Plants of Central North America for Food and Medicine*. Peguis Publishers Ltd., Winnipeg, Manitoba.

Johnston, Alex. 1982. *Plants and the Blackfoot*. Natural History Occasional Paper No. 4, Alberta Culture, Edmonton, Alberta.

Kavasch, E. Barrie. 1981. *Guide to Northeastern Wild Edibles*. Hancock House Publishers Ltd., Vancouver, B.C.

Kindscher, Kelly. 1987. *Edible Wild Plants of the Prairie*. University of Kansas Press.

Kirk, Donald R. 1975. *Wild Edible Plants of the Western United States*. Naturegraph Publishers, Inc., Happy Camp, California.

Kunkel, G. 1984. *Plants for Human Consumption: An Annotated Checklist of the Edible Phanerograms and Ferns*. Koeltz Scientific Books, Koenigstein, Federal Republic of Germany.

Langshaw, Rick. 1983. *Naturally: Medicinal Herbs & Edible Plants of the Canadian Rockies*. Summerthought Publications, Banff, Alberta.

Leighton, Anna L. 1985. *Wild Plant Use by the Woods Cree of East-central Saskatchewan*. National Museum of Man, Ottawa.

Looman, J., and K.F. Best. 1987. *Budd's Flora of the Canadian Prairie Provinces*. Agriculture Canada, Ottawa.

Marsh, James H. 1985. *The Canadian Encyclopedia*. Hurtig Publishers Ltd., Edmonton, Alberta.

Michael, Pamela. 1986. *A Country Harvest*. Peerage Books, London, United Kingdom.

Moss, E.H. 1983. *Flora of Alberta. Second Edition*, rev. by J.G. Packer. University of Toronto Press, Toronto.

Nodwell, Leila. 1988. *Calgary Guide*. Published by Leila Nodwell, Calgary, Alberta.

Porsild, A.E., and W.J. Cody. 1980. *Vascular Plants of Continental Northwest Territories, Canada*. National Museums of Canada, Ottawa.

Provincial Museum of Alberta. 1975. *Living with the Land*. Edmonton, Alberta.

Rogers, Dilwyn J. 1980. *Edible, Medicinal, Useful and Poisonous Wild Plants of the Great Northern Plains - South Dakota Region*. Buechel Memorial Lakota Museum, St. Francis, South Dakota.

Scoggan, H.J. 1978–79. *The Flora of Canada, vol. 1–4*. National Museums of Canada, Ottawa.

Stevens, E. John. 1973. *Discovering Wild Plant Names*. Shire Publications Ltd., Bucks, United Kingdom.

Sweet, Muriel. 1962. *Common Edible and Useful Plants*. Naturegraph Co., Hearldsburg, California.

Szczawinski, Adam F., and Nancy J. Turner. 1978. *Edible Garden Weeds*. National Museum of Canada, Ottawa.

Tanaka, Tyozaburo. 1976. *Tanaka's Cyclopedia of Edible Plants of the World*. Keigaka Publishing Company, Tokyo, Japan.

Tomikel, John. 1976. *Edible Wild Plants of Eastern United States and Canada*. Allecheny Press, California, Pennsylvania.

Turner, Nancy J., and Adam F. Szczawinski. 1978. *Wild Coffee and Tea Substitutes of Canada*. National Museum of Natural Sciences, Ottawa.

Turner, Nancy J., and Adam F. Szczawinski. 1979. *Edible Wild Fruits and Nuts of Canada*. National Museum of Man, Ottawa.

Vance, F.R., J.R. Jowsey and J.S. MacLean. 1977. *Wildflowers Across the Prairies*. Western Producer Prairie Books, Saskatoon.

Walker, Marilyn. 1984. *Harvesting the Northern Wild*. Outcrop Ltd., Yellowknife, Northwest Territories, Canada.

Index to Common and Scientific Names

About the Authors

France Royer

Richard Dickinson

*R*ichard Dickinson and France Royer have been working together since 1989. Richard graduated from the University of Alberta with a B.Sc. in Physical Geography, while France is a self-taught photographer. Together they operate a botanical and photographic service company.

Both authors live and work in Edmonton. When they are not working, Richard and France both enjoy traveling and exploring the diverse plant habitats of western Canada.

Richard and France co-wrote *Wildflowers of Edmonton and Central Alberta,* the companion to this volume. They have further writing projects planned.

Wildflowers of Edmonton and Central Alberta

*T*his richly photo-illustrated companion to *Wildflowers of Calgary and Southern Alberta* covers the aspen parkland, prairie grassland and boreal mixed-wood forest from Red Deer north to Fort McMurray and from Edson to Lloydminister.

Featuring more than 200 colour photographs, line illustrations, complete descriptions for over 100 plant species, identification keys and glossary, *Wildfowers of Edmonton and Central Alberta* is a handy field guide for beginner and intermediate naturalists.

Anyone who hikes, bikes, walks or travels through central Alberta will enjoy this friendly, easy-to-use guidebook.

225 colour photos; $14.95; 0–88864–282–3
At booksellers everywhere, or call The University of Alberta Press at (403) 492-3662.